Simple Vegetarian Slow Cooker Recipes for Busy People

Darci C. Alvarez

All rights reserved.

Copyright © 2024 Darci C. Alvarez

Simple Vegetarian Slow Cooker Recipes for Busy People : Effortless Meatless Meals for Hectic Schedules: Vegetarian Slow Cooker Delights

Funny helpful tips:

Nurture mutual friendships; they offer a shared social circle and support.

Your essence is a light; let it shine brightly, guiding and uplifting others.

Introduction

This book emphasizing the joy and health benefits of sharing vegan meals as a couple. The cookbook features a variety of recipes designed for two people, spanning from breakfast to dessert, with a focus on healthy and flavorful plant-based ingredients.

In the section dedicated to "Breakfast And Brunch," readers can explore creative morning options like "Breakfast Quinoa Bowls," offering a nutritious and satisfying start to the day. Moving on to heartier fare, "Soups, Stews, And Chilis" present comforting dishes such as "Butternut Squash Soup" and "Tomato-basil Bisque," perfect for cozy meals together.

The cookbook's "Hearty Mains" section offers substantial yet wholesome dishes tailored for two individuals. From the simplicity of "Spaghetti Squash Marinara" to the complexity of "Quinoa And Veggie Stuffed Peppers," these recipes showcase the versatility of vegan cooking in creating satisfying meals.

For those craving bold flavors, "Bbq Jackfruit" presents a tantalizing option that mimics the taste and texture of traditional barbecue without the meat. Finally, no meal is complete without a sweet treat, and the "Desserts" section delivers with delectable options to satisfy any sweet tooth.

To simplify meal preparation and enhance convenience, "Batched Basics" provides recipes for essentials like "Bbq Boss Sauce" and "Slow-cooked Quinoa," allowing couples to prepare staple ingredients ahead of time for use in various dishes throughout the week.

Overall, this book offers a delightful collection of recipes tailored for couples seeking to embrace a vegan lifestyle together, emphasizing health, flavor, and the joy of sharing delicious meals.

Contents

CHAPTER 1 EATING VEGAN, TOGETHER ... 1

CHAPTER 2 BREAKFAST AND BRUNCH ... 19

BREAKFAST QUINOA BOWLS ... 46

CHAPTER 3 SOUPS, STEWS, AND CHILIS ... 53

BUTTERNUT SQUASH SOUP ... 79

TOMATO-BASIL BISQUE ... 91

CHAPTER 4 HEARTY MAINS ... 100

SPAGHETTI SQUASH MARINARA ... 102

QUINOA AND VEGGIE STUFFED PEPPERS ... 104

BBQ JACKFRUIT ... 114

CHAPTER 5 DESSERTS ... 146

CHAPTER 6 BATCHED BASICS ... 170

BBQ BOSS SAUCE ... 191

SLOW-COOKED QUINOA ... 193

CHAPTER 1 EATING VEGAN, TOGETHER

Whether you're new to veganism, slow cooking, or both, this is the book for you! In this first chapter, you'll learn everything you need to know about vegan slow cooking, from money-saving grocery store hacks for vegan staples to the settings available on your slow cooker. I'll be with you every step of the way so that you can be confident your vegan meals turn out delicious every time.

THE BENEFITS OF VEGANISM

Welcome to your go-to guide on vegan meals for two! Before we dive into the slow cooking portion of the book, let's talk a little bit about veganism, starting with some of its most common benefits.

VEGAN MEALS ARE OFTEN LESS EXPENSIVE. Some of the most expensive food items at the grocery store are animal proteins. When eating vegan, you don't buy costly animal proteins for the main event in your meal. Instead, you use more cost-effective choices such as beans, tofu, and lentils, as well as other nutritious plant proteins.

STAPLE VEGAN INGREDIENTS LAST LONGER. Nothing feels better than stocking your pantry with items that take forever to go bad—it's a procrastin-eaters dream! Eating vegan relies on many dry goods like beans, grains, lentils, nuts, and seeds, which don't expire as quickly as meat or dairy. Additionally, you can purchase dry goods in bulk and store them away, saving you money.

VEGAN MEALS CONTAIN MORE NUTRIENTS. Vegan meals heavily focus on vegetables, whole grains, fruits, and plant proteins. There are no nutrient deficiencies here! Each vegan meal is packed with a variety of healthy ingredients high in fiber, antioxidants, vitamins, minerals, and plant-based proteins.

VEGAN FOODS ARE MORE VERSATILE. Unlike chicken or beef, which always taste, well, like chicken and beef, plant proteins such as tofu, tempeh, and chickpeas can be used in many different dishes and have completely different flavor profiles. Because of their neutral taste, they go easily from sweet to savory. Chickpea cookie dough? Yes, please!

COOKING VEGAN USES UP FRESH PRODUCE. We all know the dreaded refrigerator cleanout where we lay the forgotten produce to rest. In small-batch vegan cooking, you don't need as much fresh produce, and it is used up quickly. Small-batch cooking creates less food waste and more money in your pocket, instead of in the trash can.

RECIPES TO TRY NOW

Looking for a specific meal to set the mood? Have no fear; your vegan guide is here!

IF YOU NEED TAKEOUT FOR MOVIE NIGHT . . . Try Tofu Pad Thai or Veggie Fajitas. These options are 100 percent better than a delivery app anyway.

IF IT'S A CRISP FALL NIGHT . . . Cozy up with a nice fall favorite. You can't go wrong with Butternut Squash Soup or Pumpkin-Chickpea Curry.

IF YOU NEED AN EASY DINNER THAT WILL SATISFY A PICKY EATER . . . Even the most discerning eaters love pasta, especially a classic Vegan Lasagna.

IF YOU WANT DESSERT BUT NOWHERE IS OPEN . . . Break out your slow cooker and have a delicious soft Crock Cookie ready in just 1 hour.

IF YOU'RE IMPATIENTLY WAITING FOR PAYDAY . . . Round-Up Bean Pot is a perfect budget-friendly option.

ALL ABOUT VEGAN

All the recipes you'll find in this book are vegan. Vegan recipes don't use meat, dairy, eggs, honey, or any animal by-products. All 85 recipes are dietitian-created, health-minded, flavorful, and won't leave your stomach rumbling 10 minutes after eating. Also, contrary to popular belief, vegan meals are *not* inherently bland or unsatisfying; in fact, each recipe lets you try a new spice, vegetable, or flavor combination. You can start slowly by incorporating a meal or two into your weekly meal planning, then ramp it up over time. I promise planning out which delicious meal to make next will make you a believer.

Balancing Act

Don't be fooled—vegan meals are more than just salads! Good vegan meals provide a healthy balance of macronutrients like protein, carbohydrates, and fats which naturally creates a satisfying dish. Fiber keeps you feeling full longer. Adding healthy fats to meals slows gastric emptying, or how long food takes to travel from your stomach to your intestines, meaning that you'll feel fuller for longer, too. A healthy meal "pro tip" is to fill at least half of your plate with some type of vegetable. Having leafy greens on hand is a great way to add additional nutrients to each meal, especially because they go with almost everything! Throughout this book, you will discover a variety of plant-based proteins like beans, lentils, tofu, nuts, and seeds that promote healthy, filling, manageable meals.

Rethink Traditional

Don't worry about missing the flavors you love. Within this book, you will find vegan takes on familiar classics like shepherd's pie and lasagna. And yes, you can make these dishes in a slow cooker, like many other homestyle meal options. You may also find unfamiliar recipes, so get creative and try something new! If there is an ingredient you don't like, feel free to switch it up with your own substitutions. You never know what foods you like until you try them! In fact, did you know your taste buds change every few weeks? In children, they may change even more rapidly. You might like foods now that your younger self didn't like. This happened to me with blueberries, and it's been life-changing!

Umami!

Which taste do you like most: sweet, salty, bitter, or sour? These are the four common tastes that we recognize. However, umami is the fifth taste that is savory or "meaty." It comes from glutamate, not meat itself. Tomatoes, mushrooms, fermented foods, onions, and miso paste are excellent vegan sources of umami flavor. Adding mushrooms or miso paste can transform a dish from tasteless to flavorful. It may also satisfy a new vegan who misses meat-like flavors.

Spice It Up

Vegan slow cooking relies heavily on herbs and spices; spices make the vegan world go round! Cooking in a slow cooker for long periods can mellow flavors, so don't be shy with seasoning. Throughout this book, you will find a variety of herbs and spices. Oregano, cumin, nutritional yeast, and turmeric are all included to inspire your taste buds!

BUILDING ON THE BASICS

If you're like me and from a place where meat is the largest portion on the plate, vegan cooking might seem difficult. But I promise, filling meals don't have to include meat! The main nutrients in meats are protein, iron, and some B vitamins.

Lucky for us veggie-eaters, those nutrients can be found in an abundance of plant-based foods. You don't need meat on your plate for a meal to be balanced. Use plant-based proteins like beans, lentils, nuts, and seeds to get that satisfied feeling. Proteins should make up about one-quarter of your meal. Don't forget to fill at least half of your plate with some type of vegetable and one-quarter of the plate with whole grains.

Slow cooker magic starts with the staples. Use the Batched Basics section of this book to prepare staple items to build meals around. Basics aren't usually the star of the show but play more of a supporting role. They are perfect to add to other ingredients for depth of flavor and/or a shot of protein. For example, you will learn how to add Basic Black Beans—which have protein, carbohydrates, and even a vegetable—to many other dishes. You'll also learn how to prepare brown rice and use that as the foundation for other recipes. Here are some other quick reuse ideas I lean on:

Basic Black Beans > **Simple Tofu Scramble**

Slow-téed Onions > **French Onion Soup**

Meatless Grounds > **Spaghetti Squash Marinara**

Each Basics recipe will include tips on how to use them in full recipes. Even better, Basics can be prepared on the weekend or whenever you have spare time. Most recipes from the Basics chapter are suitable for freezing and reheating as needed. They're also a great starting point if you don't know what to make. Try some of these fun combinations for easy dishes:

Basic Black Beans + Herbed Brown Rice + avocado (season with cumin and lime juice) = quick burrito bowl

Cannellini beans + pasta + zucchini (toss in olive oil and vegan cheese, if desired) = easy white bean pasta

Red pepper + Slow-Cooked Quinoa **+ tofu** (kick it up with sriracha) = spicy tofu quinoa

Speedy Slow-Cooked Lentils **+ greens + sweet potato** (add vegan pesto) = root veggie and lentil salad

Onions + peppers + Herbed Brown Rice **+ avocado** (season with cumin and salsa) = fajita-style plate

Overall, the Basics section is there to enhance recipes within this cookbook and make your week of planning easier. Have these staple items on hand and ready to go during the week. If something unexpected comes up, you won't have to worry about what to make for dinner; you'll already be off to a good start.

ALL ABOUT SLOW COOKING

Now let's talk about using your slow cooker to make delicious vegan dishes. Learning to use your slow cooker is a fun, new, exciting experience, like finding a new favorite meal. With just a few valuable tips and tricks, you'll be ready to cook up a storm with your slow cooker. Here you will find your go-to guide, including tips on slow cooker sizes, options for heat settings, how long to cook ingredients for, and how to adjust the recipes in this book based on your slow cooker. This is like the little instruction pamphlet you get inside the slow cooker that gets recycled with the box—but better! All jokes aside, be sure to read that pamphlet; it will tell you about your slow cooker's unique features and if you need to preheat it. I'll walk you through some different standard features of slow cookers so you know which one is right for you.

Size

I made all the recipes in this book using my handy-dandy, $15, circle, 3-quart slow cooker from Target. This size is perfect for small-batch cooking for one or two people. In the world of slow cooking, size does matter! Using smaller or larger slow cookers affects the cooking time and results. When you change the slow cooker size, to keep the cooking time similar, choose an option that fills up to a similar level to the original recipe. A good rule of thumb for the best results is to keep your slow cooker two-thirds to three-quarters of the way full. You may need to reduce the cooking time in smaller (1- or 1.5-quart) vessels or when decreasing the total servings. The cooking time may increase in larger (such as 6-quart) vessels or if you increase the total servings.

Heat

Your slow cooker may have a knob or screen indicating the available heat settings. For this book, you only need the basic heat controls of low and high. However, each slow cooker model operates differently. Some run hotter, and some run colder. To get to know your slow cooker, perform a test run by filling your slow cooker half-full of water. Set it on low and cover for 8 hours. After 8 hours, the temperature should be around 190°F to 200°F. If it is any lower, you may want to consider a new slow cooker for food safety purposes. If it is a little warmer, you may need to decrease the cooking time. Newer slow cookers may run warmer than older models. Typically, the low setting is about 200°F and the high setting is 300°F. Keep a close eye on your slow cooker when you first start so you learn how to work with the temperature of your vessel.

Time

Manual and programmable slow cookers are the most common options. Manual cookers have a knob with four settings: off, low, high, and warm. Low and high are used for cooking, whereas warm is used after cooking and before and during serving. A programmable slow cooker has the same options but can be programmed with a delayed start time or stopped with automatic keep warm settings. Using an outlet timer with manual slow cookers can recreate this useful capability. Outlet timers plug into the wall and turn off the slow cooker when the timer is up. However, unlike a programmable slow cooker, manual slow cookers won't switch to the warm setting; they turn off completely.

GOLDEN RULES

Here are some of the best practices for using a slow cooker so you can cook with confidence. You will also likely discover some of your own tips and tricks along the way through trial and error. Some mistakes lead to new masterpieces, and some lead to the fire alarm going off! Either way, you learn something new. Read on for solutions to some of the most common mistakes made with slow cookers so you can avoid calling the fire department.

DON'T OPEN THE LID. I know the food looks good but try your best to keep the lid shut. Opening the lid should be strictly to stir or add ingredients like pasta or noodles, usually 30 to 45 minutes before the cooking time ends. Each time the lid opens, you'll need to add 15 to 20 minutes to the cooking time.

TWO-FOR-ONE SPECIAL. Use a few sheets of tin foil to act as a divider before lining each side of the slow cooker. Once you make sure it's secure, pour the ingredients in. This hack is perfect for game days like Super Bowl Sunday to make two dips with ease or when you want to cook a side and protein simultaneously.

SAVOR THE FLAVOR. Let those flavors marry! Letting a meal sit for a day may give it more flavor. Use this trick if you're meal prepping ahead of time.

SOAK YOUR DRIED BEANS. Dried beans take longer to cook than canned beans. Soaking them beforehand helps reduce the cooking time and makes them easier for your gut to digest. Rinse the beans and soak them for 6 hours, changing the water midway through.

USE LESS LIQUID. When the lid is left on, moisture can't escape. If you happen to add too much liquid to a recipe, don't panic. Vent the lid a smidge to let the water evaporate or remove the liquid completely and heat it in a pan to create a sauce or glaze.

DON'T CRACK YOUR POT! Once your meal is done cooking, let your slow cooker cool down before washing it. We all love doing dishes right away (right?), but this one is best left to cool. However, don't leave it soaking in the sink for too long.

TENDER-LOVING VEGGIES. Any tender vegetables, such as cucumber, zucchini, eggplant, or okra, may lose their texture and turn to mush in the slow cooker. These vegetables should be added about 30 minutes before the cooking time is completed.

PICK CANNED TOMATOES CAREFULLY. Choose whole tomatoes instead of diced or crushed tomatoes unless you are using them for a sauce. If you have time for an additional step, chop up the whole canned tomatoes at home. If not, the tomatoes may break down and lose their texture.

SPRAY YOUR SLOW COOKER. Use cooking spray or a slow cooker liner to save you time and hassle after you've made a delicious dish. No matter the dish you're making, the slow and low cooking time creates the ideal situation for a ring that's difficult to clean.

ALL ABOUT SMALL BATCHES

Say goodbye to hours of meal planning each week! The recipes in this book have simplified planning and cooking. No more spending time doing math and adjusting recipes from family-size servings to serving sizes that actually work for you. This book will help make planning and cooking for two so much easier.

Smart Shopping

Our health choices are made before we even start cooking. They start when we purchase food items. This section will give you tips on vegan grocery shopping for two hungry humans. Live your best life knowing how to choose healthier ingredients in the proper amounts while also saving yourself some time. My best tip is to get familiar with reading nutrition labels and aim to purchase ingredients with less added sugar, low saturated fat, and high fiber.

PRODUCE

When buying produce, choose smaller fruits and vegetables when possible. You can find good, fresh produce at most grocery stores and farmer's markets. If you prefer produce that lasts longer, opt for low-sodium, no-sugar-added canned produce or frozen options. Canned and frozen produce are just like fresh produce picked at the peak ripeness. Both are quick, healthy options.

BEANS, GRAINS, AND DRIED GOODS

Shelf-stable ingredients are some of the best items to buy. Use the bulk self-serve bins at the grocery store to get exactly what you need. This will save money and reduce waste. Some stores even allow you to bring your own reusable bulk bags to cut down on plastic bags!

CANNED, JARRED, AND BOTTLED GOODS

Sauces make the vegan world go round! Use sauces and bottled goods to take your dishes to the next level. Before buying, check for added sugar and sodium, as these less healthy ingredients are often hidden in canned or bottled items.

DAIRY

The best part about nondairy milk is the shelf-stable options available. Nondairy milk can be found in the refrigerated section, but if you peek into the aisles, you'll find shelf-stable versions, too! Most of the time, they are packaged in smaller individual cartons. Another option is to buy in bulk to save money. Just be sure to refrigerate any shelf-stable options after opening.

Storage Solutions

Make the most of your ingredients with these foolproof storage tips. No more trash cans full of food that went bad too quickly!

TOMATO PASTE: Plop the extra paste onto plastic wrap, spread it out a little, and roll it up like a little vegan sausage. Freeze.

ONIONS: If you don't need the whole onion, chop the entire thing and put half the diced onion into a reusable plastic bag. Freeze for use later.

FRESH HERBS: Wash fresh herbs in cool water, trim an inch off the stems, and set them in a jar filled with water. Store in the refrigerator.

AVOCADOS: Keep the brown away by storing your avocado in a reusable plastic bag. You can also try adding lime or lemon juice.

GREENS: Tired of water collecting in your green's container? Throw in a cloth or paper towel to absorb the water and keep your greens fresh for longer.

BERRIES It's important to wash your fruit but wash berries just before using. Getting them soaking wet too early makes them mushy.

BANANAS: Keep bananas stored away from other produce. They release an enzyme that can ripen other produce faster.

Meal Planning for a Pair

Planning is one of the best ways to use up ingredients and reduce waste. Recipes in this book try to rely on ingredients that can be used up in a single recipe. However, creating a plan will help when you have ingredients that can't be bought in small quantities.

PICK OUT MEALS THAT USE SIMILAR INGREDIENTS. Making recipes that call for similar ingredients cuts back on food waste. Using them up in one week reduces the likelihood that ingredients will find themselves in the back of your refrigerator.

ASSESS YOUR WEEK FOR THE TIME ALLOTTED. Look at your week ahead of time. Assess what days you may have time to cook ahead and what days you may need to cook ahead for.

MAKE SLOW-COOKED STAPLE ITEMS. Don't be shy about using recipes in the [Batched Basics](#) section. A lot of those recipes can be frozen and reheated for busy days.

TAKE INVENTORY OF INGREDIENTS ON HAND. Before buying anything new, check to see what you have. That way, you avoid having five cans of the same beans on your shelf because you forgot to check. This tip will help save you money and pantry space.

CREATE A GROCERY LIST. Go to the grocery store with a list and stick to it! Buying fun extras is okay, but it can lead to excess food and food waste if it's a frequent habit.

BONUS BUDGETING

Spare your wallet! No one likes unnecessarily spending their hard-earned money, especially when there are easy ways to spend less. In the last few years, more and more "fun" processed food items have entered the market. Choosing processed vegan foods may jack up the total of your grocery bill. Luckily, eating less processed vegan foods is more economical and easier than ever. Here are a few ways to make vegan eating even more cost-effective.

BUY ORGANIC SELECTIVELY. Organic options are usually more expensive than conventional produce. However, conventional produce is typically just as good. Choose whatever option allows you to eat more produce. Additionally, if you'd like a better deal on organic, look out for store sales.

TRY OUT CSA BOXES. Check your community for CSA (Community Supported Agriculture) boxes of local produce. These sometimes come in large quantities, so to save even more, split the box with a friend or family member!

BUY IN BULK ONLINE. Bulk pricing can seem more expensive because the initial price is higher, but don't let that turn you away. Purchase dry, non-perishable items in bulk; steer clear of bulk perishables when cooking in small batches, as they might go bad. You'll end up saving in the long run.

COOK YOUR OWN BEANS. You can get around four cans of beans out of one bag of dried beans, saving you some serious money! You can also cook the exact amount you need, whereas if you don't use the whole can of beans, it could go to waste.

PLAN YOUR MEALS AHEAD OF TIME. Planning meals ahead of time will help you know what to purchase at the grocery store and reduce food waste.

ABOUT THE RECIPES

It's almost time to start cooking! Let's go over a few last tips before you jump in. All the recipes in this book are designed to be satisfying vegan meals for two adults. Each dish can be portioned out to two servings unless otherwise indicated. Forget making large batches that end up in the garbage can and say goodbye to mushy leftovers! This book will be your go-to for making easy vegan meals that don't require a lot of time, effort, or money. Check out these labels and tips to help you navigate the recipes to come.

FOR TWO: The beauty of cooking for two is using a smaller slow cooker that doesn't take up an entire cabinet or countertop. Each recipe was designed for a 3-quart slow cooker. If your slow cooker is smaller, reduce the portion size and cook time. If using a larger slow cooker, the servings should be increased and the cooking time may be longer. Remember to aim for two-thirds full for any recipe.

LABELS: These help you find the recipes you're looking for. On each recipe, you will see labels that tell you more about the recipe. Labels will help those with different dietary needs or preferences. Everyone is included here!

- **GLUTEN-FREE**
- **SOY-FREE**
- **SET-AND-FORGET (COOKS FOR 8+ HOURS)**

"USE IT UP" TIPS: When a recipe calls for an ingredient that isn't used up all the way, don't worry about waste. There will be a tip at the bottom of the recipe on how to use that ingredient efficiently.

Now, let's get (slow) cooking!

VANILLA-BERRY OATMEAL

CHAPTER 2 BREAKFAST AND BRUNCH

Vanilla-Berry Oatmeal

Simple Tofu Scramble

Overnight Oatmeal Two Ways

Good for You Granola

Slow-Cooked Pancake

Spicy Hash Browns

Golden Turmeric Milk

Tempeh "Bacon"

Chickpea Hash

Good Morning Muesli Mix

Hot Cocoa

Chickpea Frittata

Banana Split French Toast Bites

Breakfast Quinoa Bowls

Breakfast Taco Filling

Vegan Pumpkin Oatmeal Bars

VANILLA-BERRY OATMEAL

PREP TIME: 5 MINUTES • **COOK TIME:** 1 HOUR ON LOW

SOY-FREE

Oatmeal takes less time on the stove or in the microwave, but this slow cooker method gives it a perfect creamy texture that's unlike any stove-top oatmeal I've ever had. Throw this together when you wake up, and it will be ready by the time you're set to leave for the day. The berries on top add a boost of antioxidants but feel free to add any of your other favorite toppings, too, such as nuts or seeds.

1½ cups water

⅔ cup rolled oats

¼ cup full-fat coconut milk

½ cup blueberries

1 tablespoon ground flaxseed

1 tablespoon maple syrup

1 teaspoon vanilla extract

½ teaspoon ground cinnamon

½ cup additional berries of your choice (blueberries, strawberries, raspberries)

1. Combine the water, oats, coconut milk, blueberries, flaxseed, maple syrup, vanilla, and cinnamon in a 3-quart slow cooker. Stir to combine.
2. Cover and cook for 1 hour on low.
3. Serve the oatmeal with the additional berries and any other desired toppings.

INGREDIENT TIP:

Rolled oats are recommended, but if cooking the oatmeal overnight, use steel-cut oats instead.

PER SERVING:
CALORIES: 247; TOTAL FAT: 4G; SATURATED FAT: 1G; PROTEIN: 7G; TOTAL CARBOHYDRATES: 49G; FIBER: 7G; SODIUM: 8MG

SIMPLE TOFU SCRAMBLE

PREP TIME: 5 MINUTES • COOK TIME: 8 HOURS ON LOW

GLUTEN-FREE, SET-AND-FORGET

A vegan's staple breakfast is a tofu scramble. It was one of the first meals I learned to cook after becoming vegan. Tofu is a complete protein, meaning it has all the essential amino acids our bodies can't make by themselves. It is also very versatile because of its neutral flavor, which allows it to soak up the flavor of the seasonings added.

½ (14-ounce) block extra-firm tofu

1 cup low-sodium canned black beans, drained and rinsed

¼ cup low-sodium vegetable broth

1 tablespoon nutritional yeast

½ cup chopped green bell pepper

½ teaspoon ground cumin

½ teaspoon paprika

¼ teaspoon turmeric

⅛ teaspoon freshly ground black pepper

⅛ teaspoon iodized salt

1. Cut one block of tofu in half lengthwise. Crumble half the block of tofu into a 3-quart slow cooker. Add the black beans, vegetable broth, nutritional yeast, bell pepper, cumin, paprika, turmeric, pepper, and salt.
2. Mix well until combined. Cover and cook on low for 8 hours while you get a good night's rest.

INGREDIENT TIP:
There are many types of tofu, but extra-firm tofu works best here. No need to press the tofu for this recipe, the liquid cooks out, nice and easy!

USE IT UP:
Don't let your beans go bad! Use them up in Quinoa and Veggie Stuffed Peppers.

PER SERVING:
CALORIES: 205; TOTAL FAT: 6G; SATURATED FAT: 1G; PROTEIN: 17G; TOTAL CARBOHYDRATES: 25G; FIBER: 9G; SODIUM: 330MG

OVERNIGHT OATMEAL TWO WAYS

PREP TIME: 5 MINUTES • **COOK TIME:** 6 HOURS ON LOW

SET-AND-FORGET

Save yourself time and hassle in the morning by making these overnight slow-cooking oats. Be sure to spray your slow cooker or use a liner.

For the Base Oatmeal

3½ cups water

¾ cup unsweetened soy milk

½ cup steel-cut oats

¼ teaspoon vanilla extract

For the Strawberries and Cream

1 cup sliced fresh strawberries, divided

¼ cup plain vegan Greek yogurt

¼ teaspoon ground cinnamon

2 tablespoons almond butter

For the Chocolate–Peanut Butter

2 tablespoons natural peanut butter

1 tablespoon unsweetened cocoa powder

1 tablespoon peanut butter powder

1 tablespoon nondairy chocolate chips, for topping

1 banana, sliced, for topping

1. Mix the water, soy milk, oats, and vanilla in a 3-quart slow cooker. For the Strawberries and Cream variation, add ½ cup of the strawberries, Greek yogurt, and cinnamon. For the Chocolate–Peanut Butter variation, mix in the peanut butter, cocoa, and peanut butter powder.
2. Cover and cook for 6 hours on low.
3. Serve the oatmeal with the almond butter and remaining strawberries, or chocolate chips and banana.

INGREDIENT TIP:

Steel-cut oats are a must! Substituting any other oats will result in mush because they can't hold up that long in the slow cooker.

PER SERVING (STRAWBERRIES AND CREAM): CALORIES: 348; TOTAL FAT: 13G; SATURATED FAT: 1G; PROTEIN: 13G; TOTAL CARBOHYDRATES: 47G; FIBER: 8G; SODIUM: 45MG

PER SERVING (CHOCOLATE–PEANUT BUTTER): CALORIES: 306; TOTAL FAT: 14G; SATURATED FAT: 1G; PROTEIN: 12G; TOTAL CARBOHYDRATES: 38G; FIBER: 6G; SODIUM: 125MG

GOOD FOR YOU GRANOLA

PREP TIME: 5 MINUTES • COOK TIME: 1 HOUR TO 1 HOUR 30 MINUTES ON HIGH

SOY-FREE

This will be your new favorite snack or nondairy yogurt topping. Store-bought granola is typically higher in added sugar, which can counteract its other nutritional benefits. This granola is a good source of whole grains, protein, iron, and omega-3s. A standard serving for snacking is ¼ cup.

¼ cup rolled oats

1 tablespoon chopped walnuts

1 tablespoon pumpkin seeds

1 tablespoon almond butter

1 teaspoon maple syrup

1 teaspoon chia seeds

¼ teaspoon vanilla extract

⅛ teaspoon ground cinnamon

1. In a medium bowl, mix the oats, walnuts, pumpkin seeds, almond butter, maple syrup, chia seeds, vanilla, and cinnamon until well combined.

2. Add the mixture to a 3-quart slow cooker and cook on high for 1 hour to 1 hour 30 minutes.

INGREDIENT TIP:

Walnuts and chia seeds are both great plant-based sources of alpha-linolenic acid (ALA) omega-3s. These fatty acids keep the brain and nervous system healthy. Try adding a serving of seeds or nuts daily for higher omega-3 intake.

PER SERVING:
CALORIES:177; TOTAL FAT: 10G; SATURATED FAT: 1G; PROTEIN: 6G; TOTAL CARBOHYDRATES: 16G; FIBER: 4G; SODIUM: 29MG

SLOW-COOKED PANCAKE

PREP TIME: 5 MINUTES • COOK TIME: 1 HOUR 30 MINUTES TO 2 HOURS ON HIGH

SOY-FREE

Say goodbye to breaking pancakes as you flip them. This Slow-Cooked Pancake cooks itself thoroughly, so you won't get pancake guts all over your stove. Cooking a pancake in a slow cooker guarantees a perfect circular pancake! This recipe uses half whole-wheat flour to help meet your daily requirement of whole grains.

½ **cup unsweetened nondairy milk**

¼ **cup whole-wheat flour**

¼ **cup all-purpose flour**

1 tablespoon natural creamy peanut butter

1 tablespoon baking powder

1 teaspoon vanilla extract

1. In a medium bowl, mix the nondairy milk, whole-wheat flour, all-purpose flour, peanut butter, baking powder, and vanilla extract until well combined.
2. Pour the batter into a greased 3-quart slow cooker and cook on high for 1 hour 30 minutes to 2 hours, until a toothpick inserted in the center comes out clean.

INGREDIENT TIP:

If you don't have whole-wheat flour, you can use all-purpose flour. But if you don't have all-purpose flour, using all whole-wheat flour may make a dense pancake.

PER SERVING:
CALORIES:186; TOTAL FAT: 6G; SATURATED FAT: 1G; PROTEIN: 7G; TOTAL CARBOHYDRATES: 27G; FIBER: 3G; SODIUM: 595MG

SPICY HASH BROWNS

PREP TIME: 10 MINUTES • **COOK TIME:** 4 HOURS ON LOW

GLUTEN-FREE, SOY-FREE

Turn the heat up! These Spicy Hash Browns are a sizzling side for any breakfast food—pancakes, tofu scramble, frittata—you put on the plate. If you crave even more spice, drizzle hot sauce over top before serving. Making hash browns in a slow cooker is a healthy alternative to frying them in a skillet. Whip these up when the carb calling hits.

1½ cups peeled and shredded potatoes

1 jalapeño pepper, seeded and sliced

1 teaspoon olive oil

¼ teaspoon paprika

1/16 teaspoon cayenne pepper

- Mix the shredded potatoes, jalapeño, olive oil, paprika, and cayenne in a 3-quart slow cooker and cook on low for 4 hours.

INGREDIENT TIP:

For crispier hash browns, rinse your potatoes in cold water then drain them thoroughly. Repeat this process a few times, then pat them dry before putting them in the slow cooker.

PER SERVING:
CALORIES:110; TOTAL FAT: 2G; SATURATED FAT: 0G; PROTEIN: 2G; TOTAL CARBOHYDRATES: 20G; FIBER: 3G; SODIUM: 7MG

GOLDEN TURMERIC MILK

PREP TIME: 5 MINUTES • COOK TIME: 1 HOUR ON HIGH

GLUTEN-FREE, SOY-FREE

Traditional Indian *haldi doodh,* or golden milk, is made with a small amount of piping hot milk and enough turmeric to make it bright yellow. Versions like this one are admittedly Westernized, but delicious and warming nonetheless. The active ingredient in turmeric is curcumin, which has been shown to reduce inflammation, so cozy up to your health!

---

2 cups unsweetened nondairy milk

1 cinnamon stick

1 teaspoon turmeric powder

1 teaspoon vanilla extract

⅛ teaspoon ground ginger

Pinch freshly ground black pepper

1. Mix the milk, cinnamon stick, turmeric, vanilla, ginger, and pepper in a 3-quart slow cooker using a whisk.
2. Cook on high for 1 hour. Once done, remove the cinnamon stick. Be careful not to spill because the milk may stain your light colored clothes or dish towels.

INGREDIENT TIP:

Adding black pepper to turmeric helps activate the curcumin. Be sure to mix well with a whisk prior to heating.

PER SERVING:
CALORIES: 91; TOTAL FAT: 4G; SATURATED FAT: 1G; PROTEIN: 7G; TOTAL CARBOHYDRATES: 5G; FIBER: 1G; SODIUM: 86MG

TEMPEH "BACON"

PREP TIME: 10 MINUTES • **COOK TIME:** 3 HOURS TO 3 HOURS 30 MINUTES ON HIGH

The next time someone asks you if you miss bacon, serve them a plate of this mouthwatering tempeh "bacon." Tempeh is a soy-based protein with all nine essential amino acids. It is made using fermented soybeans. Any fermented food can be beneficial to gut health. Use this "bacon" on a kale salad, inside a BLT, or as a breakfast side dish. I can almost guarantee it will make you a convert.

---

2 tablespoons soy sauce

1 tablespoon maple syrup

1 teaspoon liquid smoke

1 teaspoon paprika

½ teaspoon minced garlic

⅛ teaspoon freshly ground black pepper

4 ounces tempeh, cut into ¼-inch-thick slices

1. In a small bowl, mix the soy sauce, maple syrup, liquid smoke, paprika, garlic, and pepper.
2. Add the sliced tempeh to the bowl and coat evenly.
3. Make one even layer of tempeh across the bottom of the slow cooker and pour the additional liquid over top.

4. Cook on high for 3 hours to 3 hours 30 minutes.

INGREDIENT TIP:
If you feel tempeh is too bitter for you, try boiling it in water for 10 minutes. Then, prepare the tempeh as directed.

USE IT UP:
Use the extra tempeh to make [Pumpkin Chili with Tempeh](#).

PER SERVING:
CALORIES: 148; TOTAL FAT: 6G; SATURATED FAT: 1G; PROTEIN: 12G; TOTAL CARBOHYDRATES: 14G; FIBER: 1G; SODIUM: 886MG

CHICKPEA HASH

PREP TIME: 10 MINUTES • COOK TIME: 4 TO 5 HOURS ON LOW

GLUTEN-FREE, SOY-FREE

Hash was originally made to use up leftovers. The best part of hash is you can add anything to it, and it still turns out! A good rule of thumb is if you can add more veggies, do it! Fresh chopped parsley or chopped scallions make an excellent topping for this dish.

---

1 cup peeled and diced red potatoes

½ cup low-sodium chickpeas, drained and rinsed

½ cup raw baby spinach

¼ cup chopped green bell pepper

¼ cup chopped cauliflower

2 tablespoons chopped red onion

1 teaspoon ground cumin

1 teaspoon paprika

1 teaspoon olive oil

1. Mix the potatoes, chickpeas, spinach, bell pepper, cauliflower, onions, cumin, paprika, and olive oil in a 3-quart slow cooker until well coated.

2. Cook on low for 4 to 5 hours, or until the potatoes are tender.

INGREDIENT TIP:

Almost everyone needs an extra boost of fiber. Keeping the skin on the potatoes increases the total amount of dietary fiber.

USE IT UP:

Leftover chickpeas? Prepare some Chickpea Noodle Soup this week. You can add any extra spinach in there, too!

PER SERVING:
CALORIES: 160; TOTAL FAT: 4G; SATURATED FAT: 1G; PROTEIN: 6G; TOTAL CARBOHYDRATES: 27G; FIBER: 6G; SODIUM: 30MG

GOOD MORNING MUESLI MIX

PREP TIME: 5 MINUTES • **COOK TIME:** 1 HOUR ON HIGH

SOY-FREE

Muesli is Switzerland's answer to granola. Unlike granola, muesli doesn't call for sugar or oil. It can be served in many ways. Prepare it like overnight oats or eat it with nondairy milk like cereal. Either way, top it off with fresh fruit. If you like a sweeter flavor, drizzle some maple syrup over it.

½ cup rolled oats

2 tablespoons sliced almonds

2 tablespoons wheat germ

1 teaspoon vanilla extract

½ teaspoon ground cinnamon

¼ cup raisins

¼ cup unsweetened coconut flakes

1. In a 3-quart slow cooker, mix the oats, almonds, wheat germ, vanilla, and cinnamon. Stir in the raisins and coconut flakes.
2. Cook on high for 1 hour, then enjoy with nondairy milk! Store the dry mixture in an airtight container for up to 1 month.

INGREDIENT TIP:

Customize your muesli. No oats? No worries. Use another grain, such as millet or sorghum flakes. No raisins? No problem! Use any other dried fruit, like cranberries or dried apricots.

USE IT UP:

Wheat germ can be used as a healthier alternative to bread crumbs in recipes such as Easy Bean Balls.

PER SERVING:
CALORIES: 278; TOTAL FAT: 9G; SATURATED FAT: 3G; PROTEIN: 9G; TOTAL CARBOHYDRATES: 42G; FIBER: 7G; SODIUM: 6MG

HOT COCOA

PREP TIME: 5 MINUTES • COOK TIME: 1 HOUR ON HIGH

GLUTEN-FREE, SOY-FREE

Once, on a whim, one of my best friends and I decided to ride a train into Chicago. We stopped at a chain coffee shop and got hot chocolate that was $7! I nearly lost my marbles when I saw that bill. Fortunately, this cocoa won't drain your wallet and is just as good, if not better, than store-bought. You can even add vegan marshmallows at no charge.

---

2 cups unsweetened vanilla nondairy milk

1 tablespoon unsweetened cocoa powder

1 tablespoon nondairy chocolate chips

1 tablespoon maple syrup (optional)

1 teaspoon vanilla extract

1. Place the nondairy milk, cocoa powder, chocolate chips, maple syrup (if using), and vanilla in a 3-quart slow cooker and mix well with a whisk.

2. Cook on high for 1 hour and drink right away. Caution: It may be hot!

INGREDIENT TIP:

Read the labels on the nondairy chocolate chips. You don't want any that contain milk. There are a few vegan-specific brands of chocolate chips to choose from, such as Enjoy Life Foods brand.

PER SERVING:
CALORIES: 133; TOTAL FAT: 5G; SATURATED FAT: 2G; PROTEIN: 7G; TOTAL CARBOHYDRATES: 13G; FIBER: 2G; SODIUM: 96MG

CHICKPEA FRITTATA

PREP TIME: 10 MINUTES • COOK TIME: 8 HOURS ON LOW

GLUTEN-FREE, SOY-FREE, SET-AND-FORGET

Instead of eggs, this frittata uses chickpea flour. Chickpeas produce the same type of savory texture and taste as eggs but are lower in cholesterol. This frittata can be enjoyed alone or served with Spicy Hash Browns or Chickpea Hash.

---

1 cup unsweetened nondairy milk

½ cup chickpea flour

¼ cup nutritional yeast

1 teaspoon yellow mustard

¼ teaspoon baking powder

¼ teaspoon turmeric

¼ teaspoon thyme

¼ teaspoon dried basil

⅛ teaspoon freshly ground black pepper

1 cup chopped baby kale

½ cup diced red potatoes

2 ounces canned green chiles

¼ cup chopped onion

½ teaspoon minced garlic

1. In a medium bowl, mix the nondairy milk, chickpea flour, nutritional yeast, mustard, baking powder, turmeric, thyme, basil, and pepper until combined.
2. Add the baby kale, potatoes, green chiles, onions, and garlic to a 3-quart slow cooker, then pour the liquid mixture over the top to cover the veggies.
3. Cook on low for 8 hours, or until a toothpick inserted in the center comes out clean.
4. Let the frittata cool before eating, then enjoy!

INGREDIENT TIP:

You can make chickpea flour at home easily. Just put roasted chickpeas in a blender and pulse until a fine powder forms.

PER SERVING:
CALORIES: 279; TOTAL FAT: 8G; SATURATED FAT: 1G; PROTEIN: 18G; TOTAL CARBOHYDRATES: 40G; FIBER: 15G; SODIUM: 724MG

BANANA SPLIT FRENCH TOAST BITES

PREP TIME: 5 MINUTES • COOK TIME: 4 TO 5 HOURS ON LOW

SOY-FREE

French toast is a weekend morning must-have. When slow cooking French toast, whatever you do, don't pour the extra liquid into the slow cooker. Too much liquid will ruin your beautiful masterpiece. To finish off the banana split, top the toast with fresh strawberries or strawberry compote.

¾ cup unsweetened nondairy milk

⅔ cup mashed ripe bananas

1 teaspoon vanilla extract

4 very stale whole-wheat bread slices, cubed

1. In a small bowl, mix the nondairy milk, mashed bananas, and vanilla.
2. Dip the cubed bread into the liquid mixture, coating all sides. Once dipped, put the soaked bread directly into the 3-quart slow cooker. Cook for 4 to 5 hours on low. Discard the extra liquid.

INGREDIENT TIP:

Stale bread is a must! Without stale bread, the liquid won't be absorbed and the texture will be wrong. Need to make bread stale quickly? Leave it in the refrigerator uncovered for a few hours.

PER SERVING:
CALORIES: 267; TOTAL FAT: 4G; SATURATED FAT: 1G; PROTEIN: 11G; TOTAL CARBOHYDRATES: 46G; FIBER: 6G; SODIUM: 324MG

BREAKFAST QUINOA BOWLS

PREP TIME: 5 MINUTES • COOK TIME: 2 HOURS ON LOW

GLUTEN-FREE, SOY-FREE

A seed or a whole grain? Maybe both! Quinoa is technically a seed rather than a grain. However, quinoa does resemble a whole grain and can be classified as a pseudo-grain. Quinoa is so popular that the United Nations declared 2013 to be "The Year of Quinoa."

½ **cup quinoa**

¾ **cup water or nondairy milk**

1 **tablespoon maple syrup**

2 **teaspoons ground cinnamon**

2 **teaspoons vanilla extract**

1. Using a fine-mesh strainer, rinse the quinoa thoroughly. Mix the rinsed quinoa, nondairy milk, maple syrup, cinnamon, and vanilla in a 3-quart slow cooker.
2. Cook on low for 2 hours, then top with your desired toppings.

INGREDIENT TIP:

Any color of quinoa will work. Rinsing the quinoa before cooking reduces the likelihood of any bitter taste from the seeds' outer coating.

PER SERVING:
CALORIES: 201; TOTAL FAT: 3G; SATURATED FAT: 0G; PROTEIN: 6G; TOTAL CARBOHYDRATES: 37G; FIBER: 4G; SODIUM: 4MG

BREAKFAST TACO FILLING

PREP TIME: 5 MINUTES • **COOK TIME:** 2 TO 3 HOURS ON LOW

GLUTEN-FREE, SOY-FREE

This easy filling for breakfast tacos is made with beans and vegetables. Beans contain both carbohydrates and protein, so they keep you feeling full for longer. Try adding ½ cup of Simple Tofu Scramble to your tacos and serve on whole-wheat tortillas or romaine leaves. Top with hot sauce if you like it spicy!

½ cup canned low-sodium black beans, drained and rinsed

¼ cup diced red onion

¼ cup canned corn

¼ cup chopped mushrooms

¼ cup chopped walnuts

1 teaspoon paprika

1 teaspoon ground cumin

½ teaspoon minced garlic

¼ cup diced zucchini

Fresh cilantro, for topping (optional)

Freshly squeezed lime juice, for topping (optional)

1. Mix the black beans, red onions, corn, mushrooms, walnuts, paprika, cumin, and garlic in a 3-quart slow cooker.

2. Cook on low for 2 to 3 hours, adding the zucchini 15 minutes prior to the end of the cooking time.
3. Top with fresh cilantro (if using) and a squeeze of lime juice (if using) and serve.

INGREDIENT TIP:

Don't be shy! Add any vegetables you have in the refrigerator to this recipe. Taco fillings are a great way to use up any ingredients that have been waiting for their debut. The more veggies, the better.

PER SERVING:
CALORIES: 190; TOTAL FAT: 11G; SATURATED FAT: 1G; PROTEIN: 8G; TOTAL CARBOHYDRATES: 20G; FIBER: 6G; SODIUM: 9MG

VEGAN PUMPKIN OATMEAL BARS

PREP TIME: 5 MINUTES • COOK TIME: 1 TO 2 HOURS ON LOW

SOY-FREE

Oatmeal bars are a healthy breakfast that can be made the night before and taken with you. These vegan oatmeal bars are a healthy, delicious way to get your nutrition on the move. Top them with almond or peanut butter to add healthy fat that will keep you feeling fuller for longer.

½ **cup pumpkin puree**

¼ **cup rolled oats**

¼ **cup oat flour**

2 **tablespoons coconut sugar**

1 **tablespoon molasses**

1 **teaspoon pumpkin pie spice**

1 **teaspoon ground cinnamon**

¼ **teaspoon apple cider vinegar**

¼ **teaspoon baking soda**

1. Line a 3-quart slow cooker with parchment paper to make cutting the bars at the end easier.

2. In a large bowl, mix the pumpkin puree, rolled oats, oat flour, coconut sugar, molasses, pumpkin pie spice, cinnamon, vinegar, and baking soda until well combined.

3. Pour the batter into the lined slow cooker and evenly distribute it across the bottom. Cook on low for 1 to 2 hours, until a toothpick inserted in the center comes out clean.

4. Let the bars cool completely, then remove them from the slow cooker to cut and enjoy!

INGREDIENT TIP:

On the go tip! Make these the night before and store them in the refrigerator until you're ready to eat. If you want to eat them warm, reheat them in the microwave at home or at work.

PER SERVING:
CALORIES: 220; TOTAL FAT: 3G; SATURATED FAT: 1G; PROTEIN: 5G; TOTAL CARBOHYDRATES: 36G; FIBER: 5G; SODIUM: 175MG

TOMATO-BASIL BISQUE

CHAPTER 3 SOUPS, STEWS, AND CHILIS

Pumpkin-Chickpea Curry

Simple Soba Noodle Soup

White Bean Soup

Vegan Chili

Pumpkin Chili with Tempeh

Corn Chowder

Tortilla Soup

Beefless Stew

Grandma's Potato Soup

Very Veggie Curry

French Onion Soup

Chickpea Noodle Soup

Butternut Squash Soup

Minestrone

Root Vegetable Soup

Vegan Vegetable Soup

Vegan Brunswick Stew

Wild Rice Soup

Tomato-Basil Bisque

Red Lentil-Coconut Dal

Moroccan-Style Sweet Potato and Lentil Stew
Black Bean and Corn Soup

PUMPKIN-CHICKPEA CURRY

PREP TIME: 5 MINUTES • **COOK TIME:** 6 HOURS ON LOW

GLUTEN-FREE, SOY-FREE

Although this curry is not traditional, the beautiful mix of spices will make your palate dance. On the nutrition side, pumpkin is a great source of fiber and vitamin A. On the practical side, this recipe is also affordable and easy to make.

½ **(15-ounce) can pumpkin puree**

½ **(15-ounce) can low-sodium chickpeas, drained and rinsed**

½ **(13.5-ounce) can full-fat coconut milk**

½ **yellow onion, diced**

½ **cup chopped carrots**

½ **cup water**

½ **tablespoon curry powder**

1 **garlic clove, minced**

½ **teaspoon ground ginger**

¼ **teaspoon cayenne pepper**

⅛ **teaspoon freshly ground black pepper**

⅛ **teaspoon turmeric powder**

⅛ **teaspoon ground cinnamon**

1. In a 3-quart slow cooker, add the pumpkin puree, chickpeas, coconut milk, onions, carrots, water, curry powder, garlic, ginger, cayenne, pepper, turmeric, and cinnamon. Stir to combine.
2. Cook on low for 6 hours and let that sweet aroma fill your home. Serve warm.

INGREDIENT TIP:

When purchasing coconut milk, look for full-fat instead of reduced-fat. Reduced-fat milk has water added, so you get half the amount for nearly the same price. If you desire less fat, water it down at home.

USE IT UP:

Use the leftover coconut milk to make Vanilla-Berry Oatmeal.

PER SERVING:
CALORIES: 342; TOTAL FAT: 23G; SATURATED FAT: 19G; PROTEIN: 8G; TOTAL CARBOHYDRATES: 32G; FIBER: 9G; SODIUM: 163 MG

SIMPLE SOBA NOODLE SOUP

PREP TIME: 5 MINUTES • **COOK TIME:** 6 HOURS ON LOW

GLUTEN-FREE

I jokingly call this recipe "Cell Phone Soba Soup" because the last time I made it, I dropped my phone into the slow cooker. Whoops! Definitely not an official ingredient. One ingredient that *is* official is the soba noodles, thin Japanese noodles made from buckwheat and occasionally wheat flour. Feel free to add baked tofu cubes for an extra protein boost—and hang on to your cell phone.

---

3 cups low-sodium vegetable broth

1 cup frozen spinach

½ cup frozen edamame

4 ounces mushrooms, sliced

2 garlic cloves, minced

1 teaspoon white miso paste

1½ ounces soba noodles

1. In a 3-quart slow cooker, combine the broth, spinach, edamame, mushrooms, garlic, and miso paste.
2. Cover and cook on low for 6 hours. Ten minutes before serving, add the soba noodles and re-cover the slow cooker.
3. Serve warm.

INGREDIENT TIP:

Running low on spinach and have another leafy green like kale or mustard greens on hand? You can use those instead.

PER SERVING:
CALORIES: 164; TOTAL FAT: 3G; SATURATED FAT: 0G; PROTEIN: 12G; TOTAL CARBOHYDRATES: 27G; FIBER: 5G; SODIUM: 338MG

WHITE BEAN SOUP

PREP TIME: 5 MINUTES • **COOK TIME:** 6 TO 8 HOURS ON LOW

GLUTEN-FREE, SOY-FREE, SET-AND-FORGET

White beans are underrated and often thought of as boring. White Bean Soup takes this "boring" bean and transforms it into a colorful soup filled with protein and vegetables. Soups are ideal for any time of the year and can be go-to meals if prepared ahead of time and stored in the freezer.

---

1 (15-ounce) can low-sodium cannellini beans, drained and rinsed

3 cups low-sodium vegetable broth

½ cup baby spinach

½ cup diced yellow onion

½ cup chopped carrots

1 tablespoon tomato paste

1 tablespoon dried rosemary

1 teaspoon dried thyme

⅛ teaspoon freshly ground black pepper

1. In a 3-quart slow cooker, combine the beans, broth, spinach, onions, carrots, tomato paste, rosemary, thyme, and pepper.
2. Cover and cook on low for 6 to 8 hours.

3. After cooling, store in an airtight freezer-safe container in the freezer for up to 2 months.

INGREDIENT TIP:

Any white beans will do; try great northern beans, navy beans, or even chickpeas in place of the cannellini beans.

PER SERVING:
CALORIES: 263; TOTAL FAT: 1G; SATURATED FAT: 0G; PROTEIN: 16G; TOTAL CARBOHYDRATES: 50G; FIBER: 12G; SODIUM: 383MG

VEGAN CHILI

PREP TIME: 5 MINUTES • **COOK TIME:** 6 TO 8 HOURS ON LOW

GLUTEN-FREE, SOY-FREE, SET-AND-FORGET

This recipe uses basic pantry staples and everything can be thrown in and left alone. When you are ready to eat, top your chili with sliced avocado, fresh cilantro, tortilla chips, or vegan sour cream.

---

1 (15-ounce) can fire-roasted tomatoes, drained

¾ cup low-sodium vegetable broth

½ cup canned low-sodium black beans, drained and rinsed

½ cup canned low-sodium pinto beans, drained and rinsed

½ cup corn kernels

¼ cup diced yellow onion

¼ cup diced red bell pepper

1 tablespoon freshly squeezed lemon juice

2½ teaspoons chili powder

2 teaspoons ground cumin

2 teaspoons smoked paprika

1 garlic clove, minced

⅛ teaspoon freshly ground black pepper

Pinch cayenne pepper

1. Combine the tomatoes, vegetable broth, black beans, pinto beans, corn, onions, bell pepper, lemon juice, chili powder, cumin, smoked paprika, garlic, pepper, and cayenne in a 3-quart slow cooker.
2. Cook on low for 6 to 8 hours. Once cooked, transfer one-quarter of the chili to a blender and pulse until smooth.
3. Pour the blended mixture back into the slow cooker, stir, and serve with desired toppings.

INGREDIENT TIP:

Fire-roasted tomatoes have spices like green chiles already added to them. Using these instead of plain tomatoes will add more flavor.

PER SERVING:
CALORIES: 223; TOTAL FAT: 3G; SATURATED FAT: 0G; PROTEIN: 12G; TOTAL CARBOHYDRATES: 43G; FIBER: 16G; SODIUM: 426MG

PUMPKIN CHILI WITH TEMPEH

PREP TIME: 5 MINUTES • **COOK TIME:** 6 TO 8 HOURS ON LOW

GLUTEN-FREE, SET-AND-FORGET

Pumpkin gives us mega-doses of vitamin E and iron. The tempeh and extra veggies make this chili extra-hearty.

---

1 (15-ounce) can fire-roasted tomatoes

4 ounces tempeh, cut into ½-inch cubes

½ cup chopped green bell pepper

½ cup canned low-sodium red kidney beans, drained and rinsed

½ cup canned low-sodium pinto beans, drained and rinsed

½ cup canned low-sodium black beans, drained and rinsed

¼ cup peeled and diced sweet potatoes

¼ cup pumpkin puree

2 ounces canned green chiles

1 tablespoon chili powder

1 teaspoon ground cumin

1 garlic clove, minced

¼ teaspoon red pepper flakes

Pinch cayenne pepper

Chopped scallions, both white and green parts, for topping

1. Combine the tomatoes, tempeh, bell pepper, kidney beans, pinto beans, black beans, sweet potatoes, pumpkin puree, green chiles, chili powder, cumin, garlic, red pepper flakes, and cayenne in a 3-quart slow cooker.
2. Cook on low for 6 to 8 hours. If desired, blend some of the chili until smooth and recombine.
3. Serve with scallions over top.

INGREDIENT TIP:
Beans are a reliable source of fiber and help keep the gut healthy. When increasing fiber intake, be sure to increase water intake as well.

USE IT UP:
Save your extra tempeh to make Tempeh "Bacon".

PER SERVING:
CALORIES: 381; TOTAL FAT: 9G; SATURATED FAT 2G; PROTEIN: 26G; TOTAL CARBOHYDRATES: 57G; FIBER: 20G; SODIUM: 496MG

CORN CHOWDER

PREP TIME: 5 MINUTES • **COOK TIME:** 6 TO 8 HOURS ON LOW

GLUTEN-FREE, SOY-FREE, SET-AND-FORGET

The best time to find fresh corn on the cob is at the end of summer, or as I like to think of it, soup season. Blending part of the soup, as in this recipe, creates a thicker, smoother texture.

1 cup full-fat coconut milk

1 cup corn kernels

¾ cup low-sodium vegetable broth

½ cup diced yellow onion

½ cup peeled and diced russet potatoes

2 tablespoons nutritional yeast

½ teaspoon paprika

½ teaspoon minced garlic

¼ teaspoon freshly ground black pepper

Chopped scallions, both white and green parts, for topping

1. Combine the coconut milk, corn, broth, onions, potatoes, nutritional yeast, paprika, garlic, and pepper in a 3-quart slow cooker.
2. Cook on low for 6 to 8 hours.

3. Transfer three-quarters of the soup to a blender and pulse until pureed, then add the mixture back into the slow cooker and stir to combine.

4. Serve topped with scallions.

INGREDIENT TIP:

You can also use frozen or canned corn. Just check the ingredients list on canned corn for added sugar.

PER SERVING:
CALORIES: 161; TOTAL FAT: 2G; SATURATED FAT: 1G; PROTEIN: 7G; TOTAL CARBOHYDRATES: 29G; FIBER: 3G; SODIUM: 208MG

TORTILLA SOUP

PREP TIME: 5 MINUTES • **COOK TIME:** 6 TO 8 HOURS ON LOW

SOY-FREE, SET-AND-FORGET

Tortilla Soup is a Mexican-inspired soup topped with crispy homemade tortilla strips. Its base is made with tomatoes, and it highlights ingredients such as corn, beans, and jalapeños.

---

2 cups plus 2 tablespoons low-sodium vegetable broth, divided

¼ cup finely chopped yellow onion

½ jalapeño pepper, seeded and finely chopped

1 garlic clove, minced

1 teaspoon chili powder

1 teaspoon ground cumin

1 cup canned whole, peeled tomatoes, drained and crushed

1 cup canned low-sodium black beans, drained and rinsed

½ cup canned corn

2 tablespoons chopped fresh cilantro

1 tablespoon olive oil

2 (6-inch) corn tortillas, cut into ¼-inch strips

1 tablespoon freshly squeezed lime juice, for topping

½ avocado, peeled, pitted, and diced, for topping

1. Heat 2 tablespoons of the vegetable broth in a small skillet over medium-high heat and sauté the onions, jalapeño, and garlic until the onions are translucent, about 3 minutes. Add the chili powder and cumin and stir to coat.
2. Transfer the sautéed vegetables to a 3-quart slow cooker and add the remaining 2 cups of vegetable broth and the tomatoes, beans, corn, and cilantro.
3. Cook on low for 6 to 8 hours.
4. When the soup is almost finished cooking, heat the oil in a small skillet over medium heat. Once the oil is warm, add the tortilla strips and sauté until golden in color, 2 to 3 minutes.
5. Serve the soup topped with lime juice, avocado, and tortilla strips.

INGREDIENT TIP:

The oil is ready for the tortilla strips when it is shiny and moves easily across the pan.

PER SERVING:
CALORIES: 374; TOTAL FAT: 17G; SATURATED FAT: 2G; PROTEIN: 13G; TOTAL CARBOHYDRATES: 49G; FIBER: 16G; SODIUM: 200MG

BEEFLESS STEW

PREP TIME: 5 MINUTES • **COOK TIME:** 8 HOURS ON LOW

GLUTEN-FREE, SOY-FREE, SET-AND-FORGET

I used to love beef before going vegan and beef stew was a family favorite. I wanted to create a beefless version that tasted just as good. Large chunks of everything are a must to get the texture just right.

1½ cups low-sodium vegetable broth

¼ cup diced yellow onion

¼ cup chopped portobello mushrooms

¼ cup chopped potatoes (with skin)

¼ cup chopped celery

¼ cup chopped carrots

1 tablespoon tomato paste

2 teaspoons Italian seasoning

1 teaspoon dried rosemary

½ teaspoon paprika

½ teaspoon minced garlic

¼ cup frozen green peas

1. Place the vegetable broth, onions, mushrooms, potatoes, celery, carrots, tomato paste, Italian seasoning, rosemary, paprika, and garlic in a 3-quart slow cooker. Cook on low for 8 hours.
2. Fifteen to twenty minutes before the end of cooking, stir in the frozen peas and continue cooking until heated through.
3. Serve warm.

INGREDIENT TIP:

Portobello mushrooms can be used as a meat substitute in soups and stews because of their umami flavor and meat-like texture.

PER SERVING:
CALORIES: 64; TOTAL FAT: 0G; SATURATED FAT: 0G; PROTEIN: 2G; TOTAL CARBOHYDRATES: 14G; FIBER: 3G; SODIUM: 281MG

GRANDMA'S POTATO SOUP

PREP TIME: 5 MINUTES • COOK TIME: 6 TO 8 HOURS ON LOW

GLUTEN-FREE, SOY-FREE, SET-AND-FORGET

Potato soup was a classic in my home growing up. My grandma made this soup on occasion in cooler months, so it was always like a hug in a cup to me after playing in the snow or sledding. Her recipe is simple, flavorful, and made with love. Love is the secret family ingredient, so don't forget it!. Try topping this soup with chopped scallions to add brightness.

1¾ cups nondairy milk

1½ cups peeled and diced russet potatoes

¼ cup nutritional yeast

1 tablespoon olive oil

¼ teaspoon celery salt

¼ teaspoon freshly ground black pepper

1. Combine the milk, potatoes, nutritional yeast, olive oil, celery salt, and pepper in a 3-quart slow cooker.
2. Cook on low for 6 to 8 hours, or until the potatoes are tender.
3. Use a potato masher or immersion blender to mash the potatoes into the soup. Serve warm.

INGREDIENT TIP:

Peeling the potatoes is optional. Keeping the skin on adds more fiber, while removing the skin creates a smoother texture.

USE IT UP:

Use any extra potatoes in Mushroom and Lentil Shepherd's Pie or Mashed Potatoes.

PER SERVING:
CALORIES: 250; TOTAL FAT: 10G; SATURATED FAT: 1G; PROTEIN: 13G; TOTAL CARBOHYDRATES: 26G; FIBER: 3G; SODIUM: 112MG

VERY VEGGIE CURRY

PREP TIME: 5 MINUTES • **COOK TIME:** 8 HOURS ON LOW

GLUTEN-FREE, SET-AND-FORGET

Very Veggie Curry is an Indian-inspired dish full of flavor—and of course vegetables. This recipe would be a great way to use up any CSA vegetables you may have. If you're looking for an extra protein boost, serve with baked tofu cubes or edamame.

½ cup full-fat coconut milk

½ cup chopped green beans

¼ cup diced white onion

¼ cup diced eggplant

¼ cup peeled and diced sweet potatoes

2 tablespoons red chili paste

1 tablespoon ground ginger

1 teaspoon curry powder

½ teaspoon turmeric

½ teaspoon ground cumin

Rice or rice noodles, for serving

1. In a 3-quart slow cooker, combine the coconut milk, green beans, onions, eggplant, sweet potatoes, red chili paste, ground ginger, curry powder, turmeric, and cumin.

2. Cook for 8 hours on low.
3. Serve over rice or rice noodles.

INGREDIENT TIP:

Choose fresh green beans, if possible. If you can't use fresh, stir in canned or frozen beans 15 minutes before the cooking time is up.

USE IT UP:

Extra eggplant? Try it in Minestrone.

PER SERVING:
CALORIES: 187; TOTAL FAT: 14G; SATURATED FAT: 11G; PROTEIN: 4G; TOTAL CARBOHYDRATES: 17G; FIBER: 6G; SODIUM: 252MG

FRENCH ONION SOUP

PREP TIME: 5 MINUTES • **COOK TIME:** 8 TO 10 HOURS ON LOW

SOY-FREE, SET-AND-FORGET

One of the easiest soups to make in a slow cooker is French Onion Soup. This would be a perfect meal choice after making a batch of my Slow-téed Onions. Caramelized onions give the soup its rich flavor. You don't even need to clean the slow cooker; just toss all the soup ingredients in on top of the onions to maximize their flavor.

1½ cups Slow-téed Onions

1½ cups low-sodium vegetable broth

2 tablespoons white cooking wine

1 garlic clove, minced

¼ teaspoon dried thyme

1 bay leaf

2 (1-inch-thick) baguette slices

1. Combine the onions, vegetable broth, cooking wine, garlic, thyme, and bay leaf in a 3-quart slow cooker.
2. Cook on low for 8 to 10 hours.
3. Remove the bay leaf and serve with baguette slices on top.

INGREDIENT TIP:

White cooking wine is a dry white wine. You can find it at the store labeled "white cooking wine," or use your favorite dry white wine instead.

PER SERVING:
CALORIES: 349; TOTAL FAT: 9G; SATURATED FAT: 1G; PROTEIN: 10G; TOTAL CARBOHYDRATES: 59G; FIBER: 5G; SODIUM: 519MG

CHICKPEA NOODLE SOUP

PREP TIME: 5 MINUTES • **COOK TIME:** 6 TO 7 HOURS ON LOW

SOY-FREE

Chickpea Noodle Soup is so comforting on the days you're feeling under the weather. Because this is a slow-cooked recipe, there's no need to stand in the kitchen stirring and waiting around. And if you line your slow cooker, there won't even be any dishes to do. I call that a win-win. Just throw everything into the slow cooker and go back to bed.

2½ cups low-sodium vegetable broth

1 cup thinly sliced carrots

1 cup chopped celery

¾ cup canned low-sodium chickpeas, drained and rinsed

⅔ cup chopped yellow onion

1 garlic clove, minced

1 bay leaf

1 teaspoon chopped fresh cilantro leaves

½ teaspoon ground ginger

½ teaspoon turmeric powder

⅛ teaspoon freshly ground black pepper

2½ ounces whole-wheat pasta

1. Combine the broth, carrots, celery, chickpeas, onions, garlic, bay leaf, cilantro, ginger, turmeric, and pepper in a 3-quart slow cooker.
2. Cook on low for 6 to 7 hours, adding the pasta 15 minutes before serving.
3. Remove the bay leaf before serving and enjoy.

INGREDIENT TIP:

Turmeric and ginger are great for boosting immunity. Keep your immune system in tip-top shape year-round, not just during cold and flu season.

PER SERVING:
CALORIES: 287; TOTAL FAT: 2G; SATURATED FAT: 0G; PROTEIN: 12G; TOTAL CARBOHYDRATES: 58G; FIBER: 11G; SODIUM: 93MG

BUTTERNUT SQUASH SOUP

PREP TIME: 10 MINUTES • **COOK TIME:** 6 TO 8 HOURS ON LOW

GLUTEN-FREE, SOY-FREE, SET-AND-FORGET

Butternut Squash Soup is a thick, rich soup with a lot of flavor. Butternut squash also contains a ton of vitamin A. Any bright orange or red vegetable is usually high in vitamin A. This soup is easy to make and pairs well with holiday meals. I'm looking at you, Thanksgiving.

---

4 cups peeled and cubed butternut squash

2 cups low-sodium vegetable broth

½ cup chopped carrots

¼ cup diced yellow onion

1 garlic clove, minced

Coconut cream, for serving

1. Combine the butternut squash, broth, carrots, onions, and garlic in a 3-quart slow cooker.
2. Cook on low for 6 to 8 hours.
3. Use an immersion blender to blend the hot soup until smooth.
4. Drizzle with the coconut cream and serve!

INGREDIENT TIP:

Butternut squash is a fall and winter harvest item, so for the best squash selection, make this dish during those seasons. Using frozen butternut squash cubes may be an option, too.

PER SERVING:
CALORIES: 261; TOTAL FAT: 11G; SATURATED FAT: 9G; PROTEIN: 5G; TOTAL CARBOHYDRATES: 43G; FIBER: 8G; SODIUM: 58MG

MINESTRONE

PREP TIME: 5 MINUTES • **COOK TIME:** 6 TO 8 HOURS ON LOW

SOY-FREE, SET-AND-FORGET

Minestrone is a healthy soup with a heavy emphasis on vegetables and beans, although it also sometimes includes pasta. This makes it a kid-friendly vegetable dish and what parent couldn't use that? Use a smaller pasta like macaroni or rotini.

2½ cups low-sodium vegetable broth

1 (15-ounce) can whole tomatoes, drained

1 cup chopped baby spinach

¾ cup canned low-sodium white beans, drained and rinsed

½ cup diced zucchini

½ cup diced eggplant

½ cup chopped carrots

½ cup chopped white onion

1 garlic clove, minced

1 teaspoon dried oregano

½ teaspoon dried rosemary

1 bay leaf

Pinch red pepper flakes

½ cup whole-grain elbow macaroni

1. In a 3-quart slow cooker, combine the broth, tomatoes, spinach, beans, zucchini, eggplant, carrots, onions, garlic, oregano, rosemary, bay leaf, and red pepper flakes.
2. Cook on low for 6 to 8 hours. Fifteen minutes before cooking time is up, stir in the pasta.
3. Remove the bay leaf before serving and enjoy!

INGREDIENT TIP:

This recipe is best eaten right after cooking. The pasta will continue to absorb the liquid and may change texture if left in the refrigerator for too many days.

USE IT UP:

Extra eggplant? Use it in Very Veggie Curry.

PER SERVING:
CALORIES: 251; TOTAL FAT: 2G; SATURATED FAT: 0G; PROTEIN: 13G; TOTAL CARBOHYDRATES: 51G; FIBER: 14G; SODIUM: 295MG

ROOT VEGETABLE SOUP

PREP TIME: 5 MINUTES • **COOK TIME:** 6 TO 8 HOURS ON LOW

GLUTEN-FREE, SOY-FREE, SET-AND-FORGET

Root vegetables are vegetables that grow underground. Growing in soil that is rich in nutrients imparts the vegetables with those nutrients, too. Root vegetables tend to be hearty and take longer to cook, so they are ideal for slow cooking. Heirloom carrots are my favorite because they are so pretty! Anything that looks pretty is easier to eat.

1½ cups low-sodium vegetable broth

1½ cups peeled and cubed parsnips

1 cup cubed carrots

½ cup peeled and cubed turnips

½ cup peeled and cubed sweet potatoes

½ cup peeled and cubed butternut squash

¼ cup chopped celery

1 garlic clove, minced

1 bay leaf

¼ teaspoon freshly ground black pepper

1 tablespoon freshly squeezed lemon juice, for topping

1. Combine the broth, parsnips, carrots, turnips, sweet potatoes, butternut squash, celery, garlic, bay leaf, and pepper in a 3-quart slow cooker.
2. Cook for 6 to 8 hours on low, or until the vegetables are tender.
3. Remove the bay leaf and puree the soup with an immersion blender or in a high-speed blender until smooth.
4. Pour into two bowls and top with the lemon juice.

INGREDIENT TIP:

If the texture is ever too thick, no worries! You're the boss around here, so add water or vegetable broth until your desired consistency is reached.

USE IT UP:

Extra butternut squash? Make <u>Butternut Squash Soup</u>.

PER SERVING:
CALORIES: 160; TOTAL FAT: 1G; SATURATED FAT: 0G; PROTEIN: 3G; TOTAL CARBOHYDRATES: 38G; FIBER: 9G; SODIUM: 106MG

VEGAN VEGETABLE SOUP

PREP TIME: 5 MINUTES • **COOK TIME:** 5 TO 6 HOURS ON LOW

GLUTEN-FREE, SOY-FREE

Vegetable soup is one of the most customizable soups out there. You can add any vegetables you want, from fresh to canned to frozen. You really can't go wrong here, unless you're my best friend who added way too much cayenne pepper and made us breathe fire. Learn from her mistakes.

---

2 cups low-sodium vegetable broth

1 (15-ounce) can diced tomatoes

½ cup diced carrots

½ cup green peas

½ cup chopped fresh green beans

½ cup canned or frozen low-sodium lima beans

½ cup diced yellow onion

¼ cup corn kernels

1 garlic clove, minced

1 teaspoon Italian seasoning

½ teaspoon dried parsley

1 bay leaf

⅛ teaspoon iodized salt

Pinch cayenne pepper

1. Combine the broth, tomatoes, carrots, peas, green beans, lima beans, onions, corn, garlic, Italian seasoning, parsley, bay leaf, salt, and cayenne in a 3-quart slow cooker.
2. Cook on low for 5 to 6 hours.
3. Remove the bay leaf and serve warm.

INGREDIENT TIP:

Always remove the bay leaf before serving. They give great flavor to recipes but are awful if you bite into one.

PER SERVING:
CALORIES: 161; TOTAL FAT: 1G; SATURATED FAT: 0G; PROTEIN: 8G; TOTAL CARBOHYDRATES: 33G; FIBER: 11G; SODIUM: 468MG

VEGAN BRUNSWICK STEW

PREP TIME: 5 MINUTES • **COOK TIME:** 5 HOURS ON LOW

GLUTEN-FREE, SOY-FREE

I've been told Brunswick stew is a Georgia classic, but tell that to North Carolinians and you may have a hot debate on your hands. Traditionally, this dish has loads of vegetables and either barbecue chicken or pork. When I lived in Georgia, I always thought of it as a meaty take on vegetable soup. Anything can go into it, but I'm partial to okra myself.

---

1 cup canned chickpeas, drained and rinsed

4 ounces canned young jackfruit, drained and rinsed

1½ cups low-sodium vegetable broth

1 (14.5-ounce) can diced tomatoes

1 cup frozen or canned lima beans

½ cup corn kernels

½ cup chopped okra

½ cup chopped yellow onion

¼ cup barbecue sauce (try BBQ Boss Sauce)

1 tablespoon coconut aminos

1 garlic clove, minced

¼ teaspoon freshly ground black pepper

⅛ teaspoon cayenne pepper

1. Using a food processor or blender, pulse the chickpeas and jackfruit to create a vegan meat substitute. Don't blend all the way; you want it to be a shredded texture.
2. In a 3-quart slow cooker, combine the broth, tomatoes, lima beans, corn, okra, onions, barbecue sauce, coconut aminos, garlic, pepper, cayenne, and the chickpea-jackfruit mixture.
3. Cook on low for 5 hours, then serve warm.

INGREDIENT TIP:

Coconut aminos can be used as a soy sauce substitute. They are similar in taste but made from the fermented sap of a coconut palm instead of soybeans.

USE IT UP:

Lima beans are too delicious to go to waste. Use them up in Vegan Vegetable Soup.

PER SERVING:
CALORIES: 447; TOTAL FAT: 4G; SATURATED FAT 1G; PROTEIN: 18G; TOTAL CARBOHYDRATES: 90G; FIBER: 19G; SODIUM: 733MG

WILD RICE SOUP

PREP TIME: 5 MINUTES • **COOK TIME:** 6 TO 8 HOURS ON LOW

GLUTEN-FREE, SOY-FREE, SET-AND-FORGET

Wild Rice Soup is a creamy, hearty, satisfying meal all on its own. Wild rice—which is actually a semiaquatic grass and not rice at all—has a stronger flavor than brown rice and is a good source of minerals. It also has more protein than any other rice. Miso paste and coconut milk give this soup a creamy texture and unique flavor.

---

2 cups low-sodium vegetable broth

4 ounces white mushrooms, chopped

⅓ cup uncooked wild rice

¼ cup diced onion

¼ cup diced celery

1 tablespoon nutritional yeast

1 teaspoon Old Bay seasoning

1 teaspoon thyme

1 garlic clove, minced

¼ teaspoon miso paste

1 cup roughly chopped kale

½ cup full-fat coconut milk

¼ **teaspoon lemon zest, for topping**

1. In a 3-quart slow cooker, combine the broth, mushrooms, wild rice, onions, celery, nutritional yeast, Old Bay seasoning, thyme, garlic, and miso paste.
2. Cook on low for 6 to 8 hours, or until the rice is tender.
3. Stir in the kale and coconut milk, and top with the lemon zest before serving.

INGREDIENT TIP:

If you feel kale is too bitter or you don't like the texture, drizzle olive oil over the leaves and give them a 3-minute massage with your hands. Massaging the kale reduces the bitterness because it manually breaks down the enzymes in the leaves.

PER SERVING:
CALORIES: 236; TOTAL FAT: 13G; SATURATED FAT: 11G; PROTEIN: 8G; TOTAL CARBOHYDRATES: 30G; FIBER: 3G; SODIUM: 52MG

TOMATO-BASIL BISQUE

PREP TIME: 5 MINUTES • **COOK TIME:** 7 TO 8 HOURS ON LOW

GLUTEN-FREE, SOY-FREE, SET-AND-FORGET

Bisque is a French word that refers to a thick, creamy soup, usually made with shellfish and a source of fat (like butter). Today, the word is used more loosely, but the coconut milk adds that luscious texture we all love. Using an immersion blender or blender is a must for this one.

---

1 (15-ounce) can crushed tomatoes

1 cup low-sodium vegetable broth

½ cup diced carrots

½ cup diced yellow onion

¼ cup fresh chopped basil

1 tablespoon tomato paste

1 teaspoon oregano

1 teaspoon olive oil

¼ cup full-fat coconut milk

Red pepper flakes

1. Combine the tomatoes, broth, carrots, onions, basil, tomato paste, oregano, and olive oil in a 3-quart slow cooker.
2. Cook on low for 7 to 8 hours.

3. Use an immersion blender or high-speed blender to blend your soup until it reaches a smooth consistency. Add it back into the slow cooker.

4. Stir in the coconut milk, top with the red pepper flakes, and serve.

INGREDIENT TIP:

Dried spices are more potent than fresh, meaning you need less. A general rule of thumb when using spices is 1 tablespoon of fresh herbs is equal to 1 teaspoon of dried herbs.

PER SERVING:
CALORIES: 181; TOTAL FAT: 9G; SATURATED FAT: 6G; PROTEIN: 5G; TOTAL CARBOHYDRATES: 25G; FIBER: 6G; SODIUM: 428MG

RED LENTIL-COCONUT DAL

PREP TIME: 5 MINUTES • **COOK TIME:** 4 HOURS ON LOW

GLUTEN-FREE, SOY-FREE

Dal is a traditional dish that is a staple in Indian households. Traditionally, dal is creamy in texture and served with rice. It can be made with cream or butter, but I get the same effect using luscious coconut milk. Serve this dish over rice and top it with sliced cherry tomatoes and fresh cilantro.

---

1 cup dried red lentils

1 cup full-fat coconut milk

1 cup low-sodium vegetable broth

½ cup diced yellow onion

¼ cup chopped red bell pepper

2 garlic cloves, minced

1 tablespoon red curry paste

1 teaspoon dried ginger

1 teaspoon turmeric

Basmati rice, for serving

1. Combine the lentils, coconut milk, broth, onions, red bell pepper, garlic, red curry paste, ginger, and turmeric in a 3-quart slow cooker.

2. Cook on low for 4 hours, or until the lentils are tender.
3. Serve over basmati rice.
4. Store in the freezer in an airtight freezer-safe container for up to 2 months.

INGREDIENT TIP:

Unlike green lentils, red lentils become soft and smooth during cooking. They also don't need to be soaked before cooking.

PER SERVING:
CALORIES: 711; TOTAL FAT: 27G; SATURATED FAT: 22G; PROTEIN: 29G; TOTAL CARBOHYDRATES: 95G; FIBER: 14G; SODIUM: 27MG

MOROCCAN-STYLE SWEET POTATO AND LENTIL STEW

PREP TIME: 5 MINUTES • **COOK TIME:** 6 TO 8 HOURS ON LOW

GLUTEN-FREE, SOY-FREE, SET-AND-FORGET

One of the best parts of eating plant-based is trying new foods! I was very much a meat and potatoes type of person. But I had Moroccan spiced lentils after going vegan, and I couldn't believe what I was missing out on. This Moroccan-style soup will surely become a staple recipe in your home, too.

2½ cups low-sodium vegetable broth

1 cup dried red lentils

1 cup baby spinach

½ cup peeled, cubed sweet potatoes

½ cup diced carrots

¼ cup yellow onion

1 teaspoon ground cumin

1 teaspoon turmeric

Pinch red pepper flakes

1 teaspoon freshly squeezed lemon juice, for topping

1. Combine the broth, lentils, spinach, sweet potatoes, carrots, onions, cumin, turmeric, and red pepper flakes in a 3-quart slow cooker.

2. Cook on low for 6 to 8 hours.
3. Transfer one-third of the soup to a blender and pulse a few times. Add the blended mixture back to the slow cooker and stir.
4. Top with the lemon juice and serve.

INGREDIENT TIP:
Create spice blends ahead of time to save time during a busy week.

USE IT UP:
Extra sweet potatoes? Use them up in Vegan Vegetable Soup.

PER SERVING:
CALORIES: 411; TOTAL FAT: 3G; SATURATED FAT: 0G; PROTEIN: 25G; TOTAL CARBOHYDRATES: 76G; FIBER: 14G; SODIUM: 62MG

BLACK BEAN AND CORN SOUP

PREP TIME: 5 MINUTES • **COOK TIME:** 2 TO 3 HOURS ON LOW

GLUTEN-FREE, SOY-FREE

Bookmark this page for days when you don't have the time or energy to make a meal. When we don't feel like cooking, we usually make less healthy choices, so this recipe will save you some trouble. Add some zucchini or any other fresh veggies at the end if you're feeling extra green.

---

1 (15-ounce) can fire-roasted tomatoes, drained

1 cup low-sodium vegetable broth

1 cup canned black beans, drained and rinsed

½ cup corn kernels

½ cup diced yellow onion

2 ounces chopped canned green chiles

1 teaspoon ground cumin

1 teaspoon chili powder

Freshly squeezed lime juice, for topping

1. Combine the tomatoes, broth, black beans, corn, onions, green chiles, cumin, and chili powder in a slow cooker.
2. Cook on low for 2 to 3 hours.
3. Top with lime juice and enjoy.

INGREDIENT TIP:

Any canned beans and vegetable mixes will work in this recipe. Don't feel limited; you're the chef and I'm just the inspiration. You've got this!

PER SERVING:
CALORIES: 206; TOTAL FAT: 2G; SATURATED FAT: 0G; PROTEIN: 11G; TOTAL CARBOHYDRATES: 41G; FIBER: 14G; SODIUM: 369MG

TOFU PAD THAI

CHAPTER 4 HEARTY MAINS

Spaghetti Squash Marinara

Quinoa and Veggie Stuffed Peppers

Tikka Masala

Round-Up Bean Pot

Easy Bean Balls

Vegan Lasagna

BBQ Jackfruit

Sloppy Joes

Tofu Pad Thai

Veggie Fajitas

Sriracha Jackfruit

Mashed Potatoes

Very Veggie Enchiladas

Vegan Not-Pot Roast

Slow-Cooked Lentil Loaf

5-Layer Dinner

Creamy Mushroom and Broccoli Risotto

Lentil Bolognese

Mushroom and Lentil Shepherd's Pie

Cajun Red Beans and Rice

Smoked Tempeh Sauerkraut

SPAGHETTI SQUASH MARINARA

PREP TIME: 10 MINUTES • COOK TIME: 8 HOURS ON LOW

GLUTEN-FREE, SOY-FREE, SET-AND-FORGET

Workday lunch just got easier. Make this marinara in your slow cooker the night before and pack it up to take with you! Spaghetti squash is an alternative to regular pasta and a great way to sneak in an extra serving of vegetables. Use your favorite pasta sauce or feel free to even add Meatless Grounds for more protein.

---

1 (24-ounce) jar low-sodium pasta sauce

2 ounces white mushrooms, sliced

¼ cup diced onion

1 tablespoon Italian seasoning

½ teaspoon minced garlic

⅛ teaspoon freshly ground black pepper

½ (1-pound) spaghetti squash, seeded

1. Combine the pasta sauce, mushrooms, onions, Italian seasoning, garlic, and pepper in the bottom of a 3-quart slow cooker.
2. Place the spaghetti squash cut-side down in the sauce inside the slow cooker.

3. Cook on low for 8 hours. Don't worry if the skin on the squash has dark spots from cooking. Let it cool until you can touch it.
4. Carefully remove the squash from the slow cooker; it will be hot. Gently scrape the inside with a fork to remove the flesh, letting it fall back into the sauce in the slow cooker.
5. Mix the squash and sauce together and enjoy.

INGREDIENT TIP:

Spaghetti squash is like magic; from the outside, it appears to be a regular squash, but on the inside it's stringy like angel hair pasta!

PER SERVING:
CALORIES: 160; TOTAL FAT: 2G; SATURATED FAT: 0G; PROTEIN: 7G; TOTAL CARBOHYDRATES: 35; FIBER: 9G; SODIUM: 74MG

QUINOA AND VEGGIE STUFFED PEPPERS

PREP TIME: 10 MINUTES • **COOK TIME:** 6 HOURS ON LOW

GLUTEN-FREE, SOY-FREE

This might become your new go-to meal. I lived on stuffed peppers for years, and they truly never get old. Yes, this recipe calls for uncooked quinoa; that's not an error. As the peppers cook, so does the quinoa. Using a slow cooker takes away the worry of them falling over and burning on the bottom of your oven.

¼ **cup water**

2 large bell peppers (any color)

1 cup canned low-sodium black beans, drained and rinsed

⅓ **cup uncooked quinoa**

¼ **cup raw baby spinach**

½ **tablespoon tomato paste**

2 teaspoons chili powder

2 teaspoons ground cumin

Cilantro, for topping (optional)

1. Pour the water into the bottom of a 3-quart slow cooker.
2. Cut the tops of the peppers off horizontally and remove the seeds.

3. In a medium bowl, mix the black beans, quinoa, spinach, tomato paste, chili powder, and cumin together in a bowl. Spoon the filling into each pepper and place them filling-side up inside of the slow cooker.

4. Cover and cook on low for 6 hours. Serve topped with cilantro (if using).

INGREDIENT TIP:

Cooking your peppers too long can make them mushy, so don't forget about them. To add more flavor, top them with hot sauce or add vegan cheese once they're ready. Yum!

PER SERVING:
CALORIES: 290; TOTAL FAT: 4G; SATURATED FAT: 0G; PROTEIN: 14G; TOTAL CARBOHYDRATES: 52G; FIBER: 15G; SODIUM: 97MG

TIKKA MASALA

PREP TIME: 10 MINUTES • **COOK TIME:** 5 TO 6 HOURS ON LOW

GLUTEN-FREE, SOY-FREE

This Tikka Masala is an Indian-inspired dish featuring beautiful flavors. Garam masala—a common spice blend—brings complexity to the dish, while the coconut milk creates richness. Serve with cilantro-lime brown rice.

---

1 teaspoon olive oil

¼ cup diced yellow onion

2 garlic cloves, minced

½ tablespoon ground ginger

1 cup diced potatoes

¾ cup low-sodium vegetable broth

½ cup canned chickpeas, drained and rinsed

½ cup chopped green bell pepper

½ cup chopped canned whole tomatoes

¼ cup full-fat coconut milk

1 teaspoon paprika

1 teaspoon ground cumin

1 teaspoon ground coriander

½ teaspoon turmeric

1 tablespoon garam masala

1. Heat the olive oil in a small skillet over medium-high heat. Sauté the onions, garlic, and ginger powder until the onions are translucent, about 3 minutes.
2. Combine the onion mixture, potatoes, broth, chickpeas, bell pepper, tomatoes, coconut milk, paprika, cumin, coriander, and turmeric in a 3-quart slow cooker.
3. Cook on low for 5 to 6 hours. When 10 minutes remain in the cook time, stir in the garam masala.
4. Serve warm or freeze for up to 2 months.

INGREDIENT TIP:

To ramp up the flavor, toss in ¼ cup of Slow-téed Onion.

PER SERVING:
CALORIES: 185; TOTAL FAT: 4G; SATURATED FAT: 1G; PROTEIN: 7G; TOTAL CARBOHYDRATES: 33G; FIBER: 7G; SODIUM: 15MG

ROUND-UP BEAN POT

PREP TIME: 10 MINUTES • **COOK TIME:** 5 TO 6 HOURS ON LOW

SOY-FREE

My family made up this recipe one day, and it stayed a staple in our house for quite some time. Even though it doesn't use many ingredients, it's packed with protein and more vegetables can always be added. Serve this dish alone or on top of a bed of greens.

¾ **cup canned white beans, drained and rinsed**

¼ **cup dried green lentils**

¼ **cup diced yellow onion**

¼ **cup diced green bell pepper**

¼ **cup no-sugar-added ketchup**

½ **teaspoon vegan Worcestershire sauce**

2 tablespoons water

1. In a 3-quart slow cooker, combine the beans, lentils, onions, green bell pepper, ketchup, Worcestershire sauce, and water.
2. Cook on low for 5 to 6 hours.
3. Serve warm.

INGREDIENT TIP:

Sugar can be found everywhere, even in ketchup! Check to make sure your ketchup doesn't have any added sugar.

USE IT UP:

Take the rest of the white beans and make a delicious White Bean Soup .

PER SERVING:
CALORIES: 219; TOTAL FAT: 1G; SATURATED FAT: 0G; PROTEIN: 13G; TOTAL CARBOHYDRATES: 43G; FIBER: 8G; SODIUM: 192MG

EASY BEAN BALLS

PREP TIME: 10 MINUTES • **COOK TIME:** 5 TO 6 HOURS ON LOW

SOY-FREE

These vegan "meatballs" are delicious with Spaghetti Squash Marinara or topped with BBQ Boss Sauce. A "flax egg"—a mixture of flaxseed and water—holds the balls together. This trick also works to bind together vegan baked goods!

---

1 tablespoon ground flaxseed

2 tablespoons water

¾ cup canned chickpeas, drained and rinsed

⅓ cup bread crumbs or wheat germ

4 ounces mushrooms

2 tablespoons nutritional yeast

2 garlic cloves, minced

1 teaspoon Italian seasoning

12 ounces marinara or BBQ Boss Sauce, divided

1. In a small bowl, mix the ground flaxseed and water to make a "flax egg." Set aside for about 5 minutes, or until gelatinous.

2. Combine the chickpeas, bread crumbs, mushrooms, nutritional yeast, garlic, and Italian seasoning in a food processor and pulse until well combined.

3. Put ¼ cup of the sauce of your choosing in the bottom of a 3-quart slow cooker.
4. Roll the bean mixture into 1¼-tablespoon balls and place them on top of the sauce in one even layer.
5. Pour the rest of the sauce over the bean balls and cook for 5 to 6 hours on low.
6. Serve warm.

INGREDIENT TIP:

Adding sauce to the bottom of the slow cooker before adding the bean balls helps keep them from sticking to the bottom.

PER SERVING:
CALORIES: 263; TOTAL FAT: 5G; SATURATED FAT: 1G; PROTEIN: 14G; TOTAL CARBOHYDRATES: 44G; FIBER: 10G; SODIUM: 164MG

VEGAN LASAGNA

PREP TIME: 15 MINUTES • **COOK TIME:** 3 TO 4 HOURS ON LOW

It wouldn't be a vegan cookbook without a delicious lasagna recipe. The slow cooker helps the lasagna hold its shape and gives you sky-high layers. Traditional ricotta is replaced with equally decadent tofu ricotta.

---

4 ounces firm tofu

1 tablespoon freshly squeezed lemon juice

1 tablespoon nutritional yeast

1 garlic clove, minced

1 teaspoon Italian seasoning

¼ teaspoon white miso paste

1 (24-ounce) can pasta sauce, divided

½ cup diced summer squash

4 ounces white mushrooms, chopped

½ cup chopped spinach

4 whole-wheat lasagna noodles

1. Wrap the tofu in a clean cloth and place it on a plate. Put a heavy can or plate on top and let the tofu press for 1 hour.
2. In a small bowl, combine the tofu, lemon juice, nutritional yeast, garlic, Italian seasoning, and white miso paste and mash well with a fork.

3. Put ¼ cup of sauce in the bottom of a 3-quart slow cooker. In a large bowl, mix the summer squash, mushrooms, and spinach.

4. Make a layer of lasagna noodles, then a layer of the veggie mixture, then a layer of the tofu ricotta, and lastly a layer of sauce. Continue layering until you run out of ingredients with a layer of sauce on the top.

5. Cook on low for 3 to 4 hours, then serve.

INGREDIENT TIP:

Don't worry about precooking the lasagna noodles if you purchase an oven-ready whole-wheat product. Toss them in raw and they'll cook through; just be sure not to open the lid and let the moisture escape.

PER SERVING:
CALORIES: 387; TOTAL FAT: 7G; SATURATED FAT: 1G; PROTEIN: 24G; TOTAL CARBOHYDRATES: 68G; FIBER: 12G; SODIUM: 92MG

BBQ JACKFRUIT

PREP TIME: 5 MINUTES • **COOK TIME:** 3 TO 4 HOURS ON LOW

SOY-FREE

No need for barbecue pulled pork; BBQ Jackfruit has the same texture, same look, and a different, satisfying taste. Jackfruit is a tropical fruit available as a whole fruit or in a can. When cooking small batches, opt for the canned option; the whole fruit could feed an entire neighborhood.

---

1 (4-ounce) can young jackfruit, drained, rinsed, and shredded

½ cup BBQ Boss Sauce or low-sugar barbecue sauce

½ cup low-sodium vegetable broth

1 tablespoon hot sauce (optional)

1 garlic clove, minced

1 teaspoon ground cumin

1 teaspoon liquid smoke

¼ teaspoon iodized salt

¼ teaspoon freshly ground black pepper

2 whole-wheat buns, for serving

1. Combine the jackfruit, sauce, broth, hot sauce (if using), garlic, cumin, liquid smoke, salt, and pepper in a 3-quart slow cooker.
2. Cook on low for 3 to 4 hours.

3. Serve the BBQ jackfruit warm on the whole-wheat buns.

INGREDIENT TIP:

If using store-bought barbecue sauce, make sure it's not a sweet sauce, as jackfruit has some natural sweetness to it already.

PER SERVING:
CALORIES: 297; TOTAL FAT: 3G; SATURATED FAT: 1G; PROTEIN: 6G; TOTAL CARBOHYDRATES: 65G; FIBER: 5G; SODIUM: 632MG

SLOPPY JOES

PREP TIME: 5 MINUTES • COOK TIME: 6 TO 7 HOURS ON LOW

SOY-FREE

Let's get sloppy! Making a mess all over the plate is a must with these popular sandwiches. I mean, they are called Sloppy Joes for a reason. Worcestershire sauce adds layers of flavor—savory, sweet, salty, sour, and umami. No vegan sauce available? No problem. Substitute low-sodium soy sauce 1:1 or a combination of half soy sauce and half low-sugar ketchup.

---

1 cup water

½ cup diced yellow onion

½ cup diced green bell pepper

½ cup dried green lentils

¼ cup no-sugar-added ketchup

1 tablespoon chili powder

1 teaspoon Dijon mustard

1 teaspoon vegan Worcestershire sauce

¼ teaspoon apple cider vinegar

Pinch cayenne pepper (optional)

2 whole-wheat buns or 4 romaine leaves, for serving

1. Combine the water, onions, bell pepper, lentils, ketchup, chili powder, Dijon mustard, Worcestershire sauce, vinegar, and cayenne (if using) in a 3-quart slow cooker.
2. Cook on low for 6 to 7 hours.
3. Serve on whole-wheat buns or inside romaine leaves.

INGREDIENT TIP:

Look for vegan Worcestershire sauce. The original version contains anchovies, making it not vegan-friendly.

PER SERVING:
CALORIES: 369; TOTAL FAT: 4G; SATURATED FAT: 1G; PROTEIN: 19G; TOTAL CARBOHYDRATES: 70G; FIBER: 12G; SODIUM: 404MG

TOFU PAD THAI

PREP TIME: 10 MINUTES • **COOK TIME:** 3 TO 4 HOURS ON LOW

This dish is a vegan take on traditional pad Thai. Typically, pad Thai recipes call for fish sauce but we'll omit that and try our hand at a scrumptious vegan version. Prior to cooking, drain and press your tofu for a better texture. Feel free to top your meal with freshly squeezed lime juice, crushed peanuts, and bean sprouts for the full takeout experience.

½ cup full-fat coconut milk

2 tablespoons crunchy peanut butter

1 tablespoon maple syrup

1 tablespoon soy sauce

1 teaspoon sriracha

½ teaspoon minced garlic

½ teaspoon rice wine vinegar

2 ounces extra-firm tofu, drained, pressed, and cubed

2 ounces dried rice noodles

1 teaspoon freshly squeezed lime juice

Pinch red pepper flakes

1. In a small bowl, mix the coconut milk, peanut butter, maple syrup, soy sauce, sriracha, garlic, and vinegar to create a sauce. Pour it into a 3-quart slow cooker.

2. Add the cubed tofu and cook on low for 3 to 4 hours.
3. Fifteen minutes before turning off the slow cooker, add the rice noodles, ensuring they are completely covered with liquid.
4. Serve topped with the lime juice and red pepper flakes, as well as any other desired toppings.

INGREDIENT TIP:

If you want a crispier tofu, pan-sear it or roast it in the oven and add it after the sauce and noodles have cooked.

USE IT UP:

Leftover brown rice noodles? Use them in Very Veggie Curry.

PER SERVING:
CALORIES: 367; TOTAL FAT: 22G; SATURATED FAT: 12G; PROTEIN: 11G; TOTAL CARBOHYDRATES: 36G; FIBER: 2G; SODIUM: 538MG

VEGGIE FAJITAS

PREP TIME: 10 MINUTES • **COOK TIME:** 2 TO 3 HOURS ON LOW

GLUTEN-FREE, SOY-FREE

Fajitas are one of the easiest meals to make, so vegan beginners start here. This was my go-to meal for almost a whole year. These veggies are a great base, and you can add almost anything you want to them. Try adding any vegetables you have sitting around or even tofu. Top it off with guacamole, tomatoes, or vegan cheese. It's that simple!

---

4 ounces white mushrooms, chopped

½ cup sliced onion

½ cup sliced green bell pepper

½ cup sliced summer squash

½ cup broccoli florets

1 tablespoon chili powder

1 teaspoon minced garlic

⅛ teaspoon iodized salt

1. Combine the mushrooms, onions, bell pepper, summer squash, broccoli, chili powder, garlic, and salt in a 3-quart slow cooker. Mix all the ingredients together until the vegetables are coated with the seasonings.

2. Cook on low for 2 to 3 hours, or until the veggies are tender.
3. Serve as a burrito bowl, tacos, fajitas, or on top of a taco salad. Or eat them plain as a nice, tasty snack!

INGREDIENT TIP:

Using iodized salt instead of sea salt or pink Himalayan salt helps get the necessary nutrient iodine in your diet. Don't worry, you don't need too much!

USE IT UP:

Don't let your summer squash go to waste. Use it up to create Vegan Lasagna.

PER SERVING:
CALORIES: 66; TOTAL FAT: 1G; SATURATED FAT: 0G; PROTEIN: 4G; TOTAL CARBOHYDRATES: 13G; FIBER: 4G; SODIUM: 129MG

SRIRACHA JACKFRUIT

PREP TIME: 5 MINUTES • **COOK TIME:** 2 TO 3 HOURS ON LOW

GLUTEN-FREE

This is for the person who feels recipes are never spicy enough. I'm giving this one three of those little fire emojis; we really may need to call the fire department. To sweeten up the spice, try adding chopped dried mango. If you don't like super spicy but still want to give it a try, simply reduce the amount of sriracha added and serve it with avocado to dull the heat.

1½ tablespoons sriracha

1 tablespoon soy sauce

1 to 2 tablespoons water

1 (10-ounce) can young jackfruit, drained, rinsed, and shredded

1. Combine the sriracha, soy sauce, and water in a 3-quart slow cooker and mix in the shredded jackfruit.
2. Cook on low for 2 to 3 hours, then enjoy!

INGREDIENT TIP:

Sriracha is a type of hot sauce made from chili peppers. If you prefer using your favorite hot sauce instead, that works too!

PER SERVING:
CALORIES: 140; TOTAL FAT: 1G; SATURATED FAT: 0G; PROTEIN: 3G; TOTAL

CARBOHYDRATES: 33G; FIBER: 2G; SODIUM: 511MG

MASHED POTATOES

PREP TIME: 5 MINUTES • COOK TIME: 6 HOURS ON LOW

GLUTEN-FREE, SOY-FREE

Mashed Potatoes may not seem like a main dish but let me tell you, when I was in middle school, I could eat mashed potatoes for every meal. Anything can be the main event if you want it to be. Serve this with seitan steak or on top of Mushroom and Lentil Shepherd's Pie for a more traditional complete meal.

1½ cups peeled and diced russet potatoes

¼ cup nondairy milk

1 teaspoon extra-virgin olive oil

½ teaspoon minced garlic

⅛ teaspoon iodized salt

⅛ teaspoon freshly ground black pepper

1. Combine the potatoes, nondairy milk, olive oil, garlic, salt, and pepper in a 3-quart slow cooker. Cook on low for 6 hours.
2. Using a potato masher or fork, mash the potatoes until they have a smooth texture. Dig in!

INGREDIENT TIP:

For an extra-smooth texture, peel the potatoes. Leaving the skin on adds additional fiber and is just as delicious, but texture-wise, it's up to you!

PER SERVING:
CALORIES: 122; TOTAL FAT: 3G; SATURATED FAT: 0G; PROTEIN: 3G; TOTAL CARBOHYDRATES: 22G; FIBER: 2G; SODIUM: 176MG

VERY VEGGIE ENCHILADAS

PREP TIME: 10 MINUTES • **COOK TIME:** 4 TO 6 HOURS ON LOW

SOY-FREE

The best way to get your veggies in is to hide them in obvious places, like inside a tortilla smothered with a delightful sauce. Not only does this dish look incredible when done, it tastes spectacular, too! This could be your new weeknight favorite because it's easy, delicious, and will leave you wanting more. If you prefer making your own homemade enchilada sauce, go for it. Otherwise, canned is fine.

---

1 cup canned low-sodium black beans, drained and rinsed

¼ cup diced yellow onion

¼ cup diced red bell pepper

¼ cup chopped summer squash

1 teaspoon ground cumin

1 teaspoon Mexican oregano

4 (10-inch) whole-wheat tortillas

1 cup store-bought red enchilada sauce

1. In a skillet over medium heat, combine the beans, onions, red bell pepper, summer squash, cumin, and Mexican oregano. Cook until the onions are translucent, 2 to 3 minutes.

2. Warm the tortillas in a clean skillet or in the microwave so that they are easy to roll. Heating them one at a time works best.
3. After heating the tortillas, fill each one with about 2 tablespoons of the filling. Roll it up and repeat with remaining tortillas and filling.
4. Arrange the enchiladas inside a 3-quart slow cooker and top with the enchilada sauce.
5. Cook on low for 4 to 6 hours. Serve warm.

INGREDIENT TIP:

If you're using 12-inch tortillas, you may have to cut the edges so they can fit comfortably inside the slow cooker.

PER SERVING:
CALORIES: 430; TOTAL FAT: 11G; SATURATED FAT: 4G; PROTEIN: 17G; TOTAL CARBOHYDRATES: 67G; FIBER: 18G; SODIUM: 657MG

VEGAN NOT–POT ROAST

PREP TIME: 5 MINUTES • COOK TIME: 8 HOURS ON LOW

GLUTEN-FREE, SET-AND-FORGET

Everyone who owns a slow cooker has made some type of pot roast before—it's like the OG of slow cooking recipes. This Vegan Not–Pot Roast will surely remind you of the good ol' pot roast days. Using mushrooms gives the dish an umami flavor that some call meat-like. Adding vegan seitan cubes may also be worthwhile if you're really missing meat.

---

1 cup halved petite potatoes

1 cup whole baby carrots

½ cup sliced portobello mushrooms

1 tablespoon vegan Worcestershire sauce

½ teaspoon dried rosemary

½ teaspoon minced garlic

1. Combine the potatoes, baby carrots, mushrooms, Worcestershire sauce, rosemary, and garlic in a 3-quart slow cooker.
2. Cook on low for 8 hours, then serve warm.

INGREDIENT TIP:

Mushrooms create the perfect savory flavor to give this dish the meatiness that a traditional pot roast has.

USE IT UP:

Save those portobellos and use the excess in Slow-Cooked Lentil Loaf.

PER SERVING:
CALORIES: 95; TOTAL FAT: 0G; SATURATED FAT: 0G; PROTEIN: 3G; TOTAL CARBOHYDRATES: 22G; FIBER: 4G; SODIUM: 132MG

SLOW-COOKED LENTIL LOAF

PREP TIME: 15 MINUTES • **COOK TIME:** 7 TO 9 HOURS ON LOW

SET-AND-FORGET

This recipe is a holiday must-have! Holiday cooking for two can pose a challenge, but not anymore. Use this recipe as your main event for holidays or whenever you feel like having a hearty, filling meal. Not only is this a throw-together type of dish, but it is full of nutrients like fiber and iron.

---

1 tablespoon ground flaxseed

4½ tablespoons water, divided

¼ cup cooked green lentils

¼ cup chopped red bell pepper

¼ cup chopped portobello mushrooms

¼ cup chopped yellow onion

¼ cup diced carrots

2 tablespoons chickpea flour

2 tablespoons rolled oats

1 tablespoon nutritional yeast

1 teaspoon dried thyme

½ teaspoon paprika

¼ teaspoon rosemary

3 tablespoons no-sugar-added ketchup

1 tablespoon vegan Worcestershire sauce

1 teaspoon maple syrup

1. Mix the ground flaxseed and 2½ tablespoons of water to make a "flax egg." Set aside for about 5 minutes, or until gelatinous.
2. In a medium bowl, combine the green lentils, bell pepper, mushrooms, onions, carrots, chickpea flour, rolled oats, nutritional yeast, thyme, paprika, and rosemary. Make sure the spices are evenly distributed. Add the "flax egg" and the remaining 2 tablespoons of water. Mix until well combined.
3. Form the mixture into a circular loaf in the bottom of a 3-quart slow cooker.
4. In a small bowl, mix the ketchup, Worcestershire sauce, and maple syrup.
5. Pour the glaze over top of the loaf, making sure all edges are covered. Cook on low for 7 to 9 hours.
6. Enjoy warm.

INGREDIENT TIP:

A "flax egg" is a perfect way to replace eggs in baking. The standard formula is 1 tablespoon of ground flaxseed to 2½ tablespoons of water.

USE IT UP:

Use your leftover dried lentils in the Lentil Bolognese.

PER SERVING:
CALORIES: 147; TOTAL FAT: 3G; SATURATED FAT: 0G; PROTEIN: 6G; TOTAL CARBOHYDRATES: 29G; FIBER: 6G; SODIUM: 334MG

5-LAYER DINNER

PREP TIME: 5 MINUTES • **COOK TIME:** 4 HOURS ON LOW

GLUTEN-FREE, SOY-FREE

This is by far the most literal name for a recipe in this book. What else would you call something with only five simple ingredients that is super easy to make? Pay close attention to the uncooked rice; it's important to make sure you've got some juicy tomatoes so that it cooks properly. This simple recipe is simply delicious.

¼ **cup sliced russet potatoes (¼-inch-thick slices)**

2 tablespoons black beans or Meatless Grounds

¼ **cup diced yellow onion**

⅓ **cup uncooked brown rice**

1 cup canned whole, chopped tomatoes, with their juices

1. Line the bottom of a 3-quart slow cooker with the potato rounds.
2. Add the black beans or meatless grounds on top of the potatoes.
3. Top the beans with a layer of diced onions and add the uncooked brown rice on top of them.
4. To top it off, add the tomatoes. Cover and cook for 4 hours on low.

5. Serve warm.

INGREDIENT TIP:

To ensure the rice cooks fully, do not, for any reason, open the lid! The condensation buildup is necessary to make sure everything cooks through.

PER SERVING:
CALORIES: 137; TOTAL FAT: 1G; SATURATED FAT: 0G; PROTEIN: 5G; TOTAL CARBOHYDRATES: 35G; FIBER: 4G; SODIUM: 8MG

CREAMY MUSHROOM AND BROCCOLI RISOTTO

PREP TIME: 10 MINUTES • COOK TIME: 1 TO 2 HOURS ON HIGH

Forget stirring and worrying about your risotto for hours. Just toss everything in your slow cooker and come back to a pot of creamy risotto that you made hassle free. Give it a try for yourself.

- 1 teaspoon olive oil
- 4 ounces white mushrooms
- ½ cup fresh broccoli florets
- ¼ cup diced yellow onion
- ½ teaspoon minced garlic
- ½ cup Arborio rice
- 1 tablespoon white cooking wine
- 1 cup low-sodium vegetable broth

1. Heat the olive oil in a medium skillet over medium heat and sauté the mushrooms, broccoli, onions, and garlic until nice and tender, about 4 minutes. Once tender, add the rice and cooking wine and cook for an additional 2 minutes.
2. Pour the rice and vegetable mixture into a 3-quart slow cooker, then add in the vegetable broth.
3. Cook on high for 1 to 2 hours, then enjoy!

INGREDIENT TIP:

Arborio rice is a must. To make risotto, you want to use rice that has a higher starch content to give it the proper creamy texture, so don't swap it out.

PER SERVING:
CALORIES: 234; TOTAL FAT: 3G; SATURATED FAT: 0G; PROTEIN: 6G; TOTAL CARBOHYDRATES: 35G; FIBER: 3G; SODIUM: 34MG

LENTIL BOLOGNESE

PREP TIME: 5 MINUTES • **COOK TIME:** 4 HOURS ON LOW

GLUTEN-FREE, SOY-FREE

No need to miss meat with this dish. In fact, you might not even realize it's missing. The combination of lentils and spices will fool your taste buds. This is another one of those recipes that lets the flavors marry over time. Serve with zucchini noodles or whole-wheat pasta, and don't be afraid to eat this in the break room—everyone will want a bite!

---

1 cup fire-roasted tomatoes

½ cup low-sodium vegetable broth

½ cup dried green lentils

¼ cup diced yellow onion

2 tablespoons brown sugar

2 tablespoons fresh basil leaves

2 tablespoons marinara sauce

1 tablespoon apple cider vinegar

2 garlic cloves, minced

1 teaspoon Italian seasoning

1 teaspoon dried oregano

¼ teaspoon cayenne pepper

⅛ teaspoon iodized salt

2 zucchini, spiralized

1. Combine the tomatoes, broth, lentils, onions, brown sugar, basil, marinara sauce, vinegar, garlic, Italian seasoning, oregano, cayenne, and salt in a 3-quart slow cooker.
2. Cook on low for 4 hours and serve over top of the zucchini noodles.

INGREDIENT TIP:

You can purchase a spiralizer to make zucchini noodles yourself or purchase pre-spiralized zucchini at the grocery store. Just heat in a pan or serve cold.

USE IT UP:

Extra lentils? Use them to make a delicious Slow-Cooked Lentil Loaf.

PER SERVING:
CALORIES: 291; TOTAL FAT: 1G; SATURATED FAT: 0G; PROTEIN: 16G; TOTAL CARBOHYDRATES: 58G; FIBER: 9G; SODIUM: 96MG

MUSHROOM AND LENTIL SHEPHERD'S PIE

PREP TIME: 15 MINUTES • **COOK TIME:** 6 HOURS ON LOW

This dish is a homestyle favorite. Shepherd's pie is traditionally known as being a "meat pie," but in meat-free cooking, lentils are a great replacement. Who says meat-free eating has to be boring or complicated? Not us!

1½ cups low-sodium vegetable broth

1 cup diced carrots

½ cup diced yellow onion

½ cup diced celery

½ cup dried green lentils

¼ cup diced mushrooms

1 garlic clove, minced

¼ cup frozen peas

¼ cup frozen corn

1 cup Mashed Potatoes

1. Combine the broth, carrots, onions, celery, lentils, mushrooms, and garlic in a 3-quart slow cooker.
2. Cook on low for 6 hours. Fifteen minutes before the cooking time is up, stir in the frozen peas and corn, then top with the mashed potatoes. Continue to cook for the remaining 15 minutes.

3. Now sit back, relax, and enjoy this easy homestyle meal!

INGREDIENT TIP:

If you don't feel like mincing up garlic, you can buy pre-minced garlic at the grocery store.

PER SERVING:
CALORIES: 250; TOTAL FAT: 1G; SATURATED FAT: 0G; PROTEIN: 15G; TOTAL CARBOHYDRATES: 48G; FIBER: 9G; SODIUM: 71MG

CAJUN RED BEANS AND RICE

PREP TIME: 5 MINUTES • **COOK TIME:** 6 TO 8 HOURS ON HIGH

GLUTEN-FREE, SOY-FREE, SET-AND-FORGET

This recipe is inspired by a popular Louisiana dish. We won't be using traditional sausage but hearty spices ensure it's still full of flavor. Putting beans and rice together creates a complete protein, which means they provide all nine essential amino acids.

¼ pound dried red beans, soaked overnight

2 cups low-sodium vegetable broth

¼ cup chopped yellow onion

¼ cup diced green bell pepper

1 bay leaf

2 teaspoons minced garlic

1 teaspoon paprika

1 teaspoon dried thyme

¼ teaspoon liquid smoke

¼ teaspoon freshly ground black pepper

Pinch cayenne pepper (optional)

Iodized salt

Chopped scallions, both white and green parts, for topping

Brown rice, for serving

1. After soaking the dried beans overnight, discard the liquid and rinse the beans with clean water.
2. In a 3-quart slow cooker, combine the beans, broth, onions, green bell pepper, bay leaf, garlic, paprika, thyme, liquid smoke, pepper, and cayenne (if using).
3. Cook on low for 6 to 8 hours, until the beans are tender. Season with salt and pepper and top with the scallions.
4. Remove bay leaf and serve with brown rice.

INGREDIENT TIP:

Soaking your beans helps reduce the amount of gas you may experience by removing oligosaccharides, which can cause gastrointestinal distress. It also helps make the protein easier to digest.

PER SERVING:
CALORIES: 320; TOTAL FAT: 2; SATURATED FAT: 0G; PROTEIN: 16G; TOTAL CARBOHYDRATES: 62G; FIBER: 12G; SODIUM: 86MG

SMOKED TEMPEH SAUERKRAUT

PREP TIME: 5 MINUTES • **COOK TIME:** 2 HOURS ON LOW

This recipe is a family favorite that my grandma swears by. Our original recipe calls for smoked sausage, but tempeh is the best alternative. My grandma said this sauerkraut-based dish brings blessings and wealth, so my family eats it every New Year. We're still waiting for the wealth, but the tradition stands!

---

4 ounces tempeh

½ teaspoon liquid smoke

1 cup sauerkraut

1 cup Mashed Potatoes

¼ cup shredded vegan cheese

1. In the bottom of a 3-quart slow cooker, arrange the tempeh in an even layer. Drizzle the liquid smoke over the top, then add the sauerkraut. Add the mashed potatoes and top with your favorite vegan cheese.
2. Cook on low for 2 hours, or until the cheese has melted.
3. Enjoy warm for good fortune!

INGREDIENT TIP:

For a more flavorful dish, use a batch of Tempeh "Bacon" instead of regular tempeh. Also, no hating on sauerkraut! Because it's a fermented food, it is great for building a healthy gut.

USE IT UP:
Turn your extra tempeh into Tempeh "Bacon".

PER SERVING:
CALORIES: 237; TOTAL FAT: 11G; SATURATED FAT: 1G; PROTEIN: 16G; TOTAL CARBOHYDRATES: 22G; FIBER: 3G; SODIUM: 369MG

GOOEY VEGAN BROWNIES

CHAPTER 5 DESSERTS

Cranberry-Yam Crumble
The Crock Cookie
Baked Apples
Chocolate-Peanut Bites
Candied Nuts
Apple Cider
Poached Peaches
Gooey Vegan Brownies
Chocolate-Banana Cake
Easy Applesauce
Puppy Chow

CRANBERRY-YAM CRUMBLE

PREP TIME: 10 MINUTES • COOK TIME: 4 HOURS ON HIGH

SOY-FREE

This recipe is a holiday must-have in my family. It has been a fan favorite since I made a vegan version of it in 2016. This dish proves that desserts can be part of a healthy lifestyle. Personally, I like to pair this with vanilla ice cream, but my grandpa loves adding vegan marshmallows!

¾ **(15-ounce) can organic yams**

4 ounces cranberries, fresh or frozen

Juice of 1 orange

2 tablespoons frozen cherries

2 tablespoons whole-wheat flour

2 tablespoons packed brown sugar

2 tablespoons rolled oats

2 tablespoons vegan butter, melted

⅓ teaspoon ground cinnamon

1. Add the yams to a 3-quart slow cooker.
2. In a small bowl, mash the cranberries, orange juice, and cherries. Add the fruit mixture to the slow cooker to cover the yams.

3. In a small bowl, add the whole-wheat flour, brown sugar, rolled oats, vegan butter, and cinnamon. Stir to combine.

4. Sprinkle the topping over the fruit mixture and yams. Cover and cook on high for 4 hours. Serve warm.

INGREDIENT TIP:

Usually purchasing organic goods isn't completely necessary but canned yams are an exception. Most nonorganic yams include high-fructose corn syrup, which is an added sugar.

USE IT UP:

Use your leftover cranberries as a topping for the Vanilla-Berry Oatmeal.

PER SERVING:
CALORIES: 443; TOTAL FAT: 12G; SATURATED FAT: 2G; PROTEIN: 5G; TOTAL CARBOHYDRATES: 83G; FIBER: 12G; SODIUM: 23MG

THE CROCK COOKIE

PREP TIME: 5 MINUTES • **COOK TIME:** 2 TO 3 HOURS ON HIGH

SOY-FREE

Calling all cookie lovers, myself included! Nothing says dessert quite like a chocolate chip cookie. Feel free to add any additional toppings you like, such as nuts or cocoa nibs. Don't forget to grease your slow cooker, so you don't lose any of the goods; trust me, you don't want to miss out on a single bite!

---

1 tablespoon ground flaxseed

2½ tablespoons water

2 tablespoons melted vegan butter

2 tablespoons coconut sugar

½ teaspoon vanilla extract

¼ cup whole-wheat flour

¼ cup nondairy chocolate chips or cocoa nibs

1. Mix the ground flaxseed and water to create a "flax egg." Let this mixture sit for about 5 minutes, or until gelatinous.
2. In a medium bowl, mix the vegan butter, coconut sugar, vanilla, and "flax egg" until well combined.
3. Slowly add the whole-wheat flour and stir until well combined; don't overmix.

4. Fold in the nondairy chocolate chips. Spread the mixture in a greased or lined 3-quart slow cooker and cook on high for 2 to 3 hours.

5. When done, let the cookie cool, then dig in.

INGREDIENT TIP:

Coconut sugar comes from the sap of a coconut tree. It can be substituted for regular sugar because refined sugar may be filtered with bone char. Look for "natural carbon" In the ingredient list.

PER SERVING:
CALORIES: 351; TOTAL FAT: 22G; SATURATED FAT: 8G; PROTEIN: 4G; TOTAL CARBOHYDRATES: 34G; FIBER: 5G; SODIUM: 89MG

BAKED APPLES

PREP TIME: 10 MINUTES • **COOK TIME:** 2 HOURS ON LOW

SOY-FREE

Baked Apples are simple and delicious. Try making this recipe from late July to November, when apples are in season. Enjoy the taste of tart apples with sweet flavors. While the apples bake, they create their own fragrant sauce.

---

2 Gala apples

2½ tablespoons orange juice

2 tablespoons coconut sugar

2 tablespoons rolled oats

1 tablespoon vegan butter

1 teaspoon ground cinnamon

½ teaspoon vanilla extract

⅛ teaspoon iodized salt

1. First, cut the top of the apples horizontally to create a flat surface.
2. In a small bowl, combine the orange juice, coconut sugar, oats, vegan butter, cinnamon, vanilla, and salt and set aside.
3. Remove the core of the apple with a melon baller or spoon so there is a hole in the middle of each apple.

4. Spoon the mixture into the holes and place the apples upright in a 3-quart slow cooker.

5. Cook on low for 2 hours, or until the apples are tender but still hold their shape.

INGREDIENT TIP:
Cinnamon is a wonderful spice to use because it adds flavor without using sugar or salt.

PER SERVING:
CALORIES: 249; TOTAL FAT: 7G; SATURATED FAT: 1G; PROTEIN: 2G; TOTAL CARBOHYDRATES: 48G; FIBER: 6G; SODIUM: 160MG

CHOCOLATE-PEANUT BITES

PREP TIME: 5 MINUTES • **COOK TIME:** 30 MINUTES ON LOW

GLUTEN-FREE, SOY-FREE

Enjoy the sweet combination of peanut butter and chocolate. A slow cooker is the easiest way to melt chocolate without burning it. These bites are sure to be a hit. Make a batch and save them to have throughout the week.

½ **cup unsalted peanuts**

¾ **cup nondairy chocolate chips**

¼ **cup natural smooth peanut butter**

1. Layer the peanuts, chocolate chips, and peanut butter into the bottom of a 3-quart slow cooker.
2. Cook on low for 30 minutes until the chocolate is melted. Mix all the ingredients together. Scoop out 2 tablespoons of the mixture at a time onto a parchment paper–lined baking sheet. Continue until all the mixture is used up.
3. Place the baking sheet in the refrigerator for 1 hour, or until the chocolate has hardened.
4. Eat one and put the rest in the freezer to enjoy later in the week.

INGREDIENT TIP:
Choosing unsalted peanuts reduces the total amount of sodium.

Also, select peanut butter with peanuts as the only ingredient.

PER SERVING:
CALORIES: 765; TOTAL FAT: 61G; SATURATED FAT: 19G; PROTEIN: 20G;
TOTAL CARBOHYDRATES: 41G; FIBER: 13G; SODIUM: 85MG

CANDIED NUTS

PREP TIME: 5 MINUTES • **COOK TIME:** 3 HOURS ON LOW

GLUTEN-FREE, SOY-FREE

Easy, egg white–free candied nuts are a tasty gift item for the holidays. Nuts are a great source of protein, vitamins, and minerals. They are also higher in healthy fats, so be mindful of portion size. Instead of lighting a candle, try making these sweet treats and let their aroma fill your home.

¼ cup coconut sugar

1 teaspoon ground cinnamon

1 teaspoon ground ginger

1 teaspoon ground nutmeg

½ cup raw almonds

½ cup pecans

1 tablespoon water

1 teaspoon vanilla extract

1. In a small bowl, mix the coconut sugar, cinnamon, ginger, and nutmeg. Set aside.
2. Place the almonds, pecans, water, and vanilla into a 3-quart slow cooker.

3. Cook on low for 3 hours. Once done, place the hot nuts on a parchment paper–lined baking sheet and sprinkle with the sugar-spice mixture.

4. Let the nuts cool and then enjoy, or store in an airtight container at room temperature for later.

INGREDIENT TIP:

Almonds are a great source of vitamin E, an antioxidant that helps keep your cells healthy. Cooking the nuts for too long may cause them to burn, so watch your slow cooker timer.

PER SERVING:
CALORIES: 495; TOTAL FAT: 36G; SATURATED FAT: 3G; PROTEIN: 10G; TOTAL CARBOHYDRATES: 38G; FIBER: 8G; SODIUM: 2MG

APPLE CIDER

PREP TIME: 5 MINUTES • **COOK TIME:** 8 TO 10 HOURS ON LOW

GLUTEN-FREE, SOY-FREE, SET-AND-FORGET

Homemade, slow-cooked Apple Cider is simple and just as good as what you'd find at a fall festival. Mashed apples create a more flavorful cider, but you'll want to strain the mixture before serving.

4 cups water

2 Honeycrisp apples

½ orange, peeled and sliced

2 tablespoons maple syrup (optional)

1 cinnamon stick

2 teaspoons ground allspice

1. Combine the water, apples, orange, maple syrup (if using), cinnamon stick, and allspice in a 3-quart slow cooker.
2. Set the slow cooker to low and cook for 8 to 10 hours.
3. Once the cooking time is up, remove the cinnamon stick and use a potato masher to gently mash the fruit to release all its flavors.
4. Strain the apple cider through a cheesecloth or fine-mesh strainer, then pour into your favorite mug and enjoy.

INGREDIENT TIP:

There should be enough water in the slow cooker so that the apples and orange are completely submerged. The type of apples that you choose will determine the sweetness of the finished cider.

PER SERVING:
CALORIES: 113; TOTAL FAT: 0G; SATURATED FAT: 0G; PROTEIN: 0G; TOTAL CARBOHYDRATES: 27G; FIBER: 1G; SODIUM: 12MG

POACHED PEACHES

PREP TIME: 5 MINUTES • **COOK TIME:** 1 TO 2 HOURS ON HIGH

GLUTEN-FREE, SOY-FREE

If chocolate desserts aren't your thing, try a fresh fruit dessert. On average, we should aim to eat at least 5 cups of fruits and vegetables each day. Peaches come into season in summer and can be a perfect refreshing dessert. You want to cook these until they are just soft; overcooking can lead to mushy fruit. Serve as a dessert with ice cream or add them to your breakfast cereal.

---

2 fresh peaches, halved and pitted

4 ounces fresh raspberries

2 tablespoons torn basil leaves

1 cinnamon stick

1 tablespoon water

2 strips peeled lemon zest

1. Add the peaches, raspberries, basil, cinnamon stick, water, and lemon zest to a 3-quart slow cooker.
2. Cook on high for 1 to 2 hours, or until the peaches are tender.
3. To serve, remove the cinnamon stick, scoop out the peaches, and drizzle the leftover liquid from the slow cooker over top.

INGREDIENT TIP:

If you want to get a little fancier, try using white wine instead of water to poach the peaches.

PER SERVING:
CALORIES: 99; TOTAL FAT: 1G; SATURATED FAT: 0G; PROTEIN: 2G; TOTAL CARBOHYDRATES: 24G; FIBER: 6G; SODIUM: 1MG

GOOEY VEGAN BROWNIES

PREP TIME: 5 MINUTES • **COOK TIME:** 2 TO 3 HOURS ON LOW

Brownies are an age-old dessert. I grew up making box-mix brownies and nurtured a love for this ooey-gooey treat ever since. This recipe is a recreation of my childhood favorite—from scratch! Try serving it with nondairy vanilla ice cream.

---

1 tablespoon ground flaxseed

2½ tablespoons water

¼ cup vegan butter

¼ cup coconut sugar

1 teaspoon vanilla extract

2 tablespoons, plus 2 teaspoons whole-wheat flour

2½ tablespoons unsweetened cocoa powder

1 tablespoon vegan chocolate chips

1 tablespoon chopped walnuts (optional)

1. Mix the ground flaxseed and water to create a "flax egg." Let this mixture sit for about 5 minutes, or until gelatinous.
2. Melt the butter in a microwave-safe dish at 15 second intervals, then mix in the coconut sugar and vanilla. Once the "flax egg" has set, add it to the bowl as well.

3. In a separate small bowl, mix the flour and cocoa powder. Once combined, add the wet ingredients to the dry ones and mix until combined. Add the chocolate chips and walnuts (if using) and stir.

4. Pour the mixture into an aluminum foil–lined 3-quart slow cooker and cook on low for 2 to 3 hours, or until a toothpick inserted in the center comes out clean.

INGREDIENT TIP:

The main difference between cocoa and cacao powders is that cocoa powder is made at higher temperatures and sometimes will contain added sugar or dairy. Cacao power is made from beans that are heated, not roasted. Cocoa powder is often cheaper, but look for "100-percent cocoa."

PER SERVING:
CALORIES: 421; TOTAL FAT: 30G; SATURATED FAT: 3G; PROTEIN: 4G; TOTAL CARBOHYDRATES: 39G; FIBER: 5G; SODIUM: 12MG

CHOCOLATE-BANANA CAKE

PREP TIME: 5 MINUTES • **COOK TIME:** 2 TO 3 HOURS ON LOW

SOY-FREE

Does banana bread count as a serving of fruit? Probably not, but we can pretend that it does. Still, sneaking fruits and vegetables into foods always has some type of benefit, such as increasing the total fiber content. You may not get all the nutritional benefits because of the other ingredients added, but it's better than not having them at all. This cake is easy and comes out with a fluffy, moist texture.

- ¼ cup mashed bananas
- 2 tablespoons coconut sugar
- 2 tablespoons avocado oil
- 1 teaspoon vanilla extract
- ¼ cup whole-wheat flour
- 1 tablespoon unsweetened cocoa powder
- ½ teaspoon ground cinnamon
- ½ teaspoon baking powder
- ½ teaspoon baking soda
- 2 tablespoons vegan chocolate chips

1. In a small bowl, mix the bananas, coconut sugar, avocado oil, and vanilla until well combined.
2. In a separate small bowl, mix the flour, cocoa powder, cinnamon, baking powder, and baking soda.
3. Add the wet ingredients and vegan chocolate chips to the dry ingredients and mix the batter together.
4. Pour the batter into and aluminum foil–lined 3-quart slow cooker and bake on low for 2 to 3 hours, or until a toothpick inserted in the center comes out clean.

INGREDIENT TIP:

Ripe, lightly spotted bananas work well in this recipe. The riper a banana is, the sweeter it will taste.

PER SERVING:
CALORIES: 324; TOTAL FAT: 19G; SATURATED FAT: 4G; PROTEIN: 4G; TOTAL CARBOHYDRATES: 37G; FIBER: 5G; SODIUM: 409MG

EASY APPLESAUCE

PREP TIME: 5 MINUTES • **COOK TIME:** 2 TO 3 HOURS ON HIGH

GLUTEN-FREE, SOY-FREE

Applesauce is one of the best snacks or desserts out there. It's severely underrated in my opinion. Desserts don't always have to be made of chocolate and be full of added sugar; fruit can be a healthy way to curb a sweet tooth, too. The apples in this recipe go into the slow cooker diced, and as they cook down, you'll be able to mash them into applesauce.

---

2 Gala apples, peeled, cored, and diced

1 tablespoon freshly squeezed lemon juice

1 teaspoon ground cinnamon

2 tablespoons water

1. Place the diced apples into a 3-quart slow cooker. Sprinkle the lemon juice and cinnamon over top and mix until the apples are coated.
2. Add the water and cover the slow cooker.
3. Cook on high for 2 to 3 hours, or until the apples are softened.
4. Use a fork or whisk to mix and mash the cooked apples until your desired consistency is reached. Enjoy warm or refrigerate in a sealed container.

INGREDIENT TIP:

Lemon juice helps keep the apples from browning. If lemon juice is not available, any acid, such as apple cider vinegar, will work instead.

PER SERVING:
CALORIES: 86; TOTAL FAT: 0G; SATURATED FAT: 0G; PROTEIN: 1G; TOTAL CARBOHYDRATES: 23G; FIBER: 3G; SODIUM: 0MG

PUPPY CHOW

PREP TIME: 5 MINUTES • **COOK TIME:** 30 MINUTES ON LOW

GLUTEN-FREE, SOY-FREE

Puppy Chow is the biggest party hit out there! But you don't have to wait until your next party to indulge; you can make it right at home. Super speedy and simple, this recipe is perfect for a pick-me-up anytime.

---

2 ounces dark chocolate

2 tablespoons natural peanut butter

1 teaspoon vanilla extract

⅔ cup Rice Chex

2 tablespoons confectioners' sugar

1. Combine the chocolate, peanut butter, and vanilla in a 3-quart slow cooker. Cook on low for 30 minutes, or until everything is melted.
2. Turn the slow cooker off and add the rice Chex. Mix until well coated.
3. Remove the chocolate-covered Chex from the slow cooker and place into a reusable baggie or airtight container.
4. Pour the confectioners' sugar into the container or baggie and shake until the pieces are evenly coated. Voila!

INGREDIENT TIP:

Great news: Dark chocolate has some nutritional value. When possible, look for a dark chocolate that is at least 75-percent cocoa. These are healthier options and are less likely to contain milk.

PER SERVING:
CALORIES: 339; TOTAL FAT: 21G; SATURATED FAT: 8G; PROTEIN: 6G; TOTAL CARBOHYDRATES: 32G; FIBER: 5G; SODIUM: 88MG

HERBED POTATOES

CHAPTER 6 BATCHED BASICS

Baked Beans
Ginger-Sesame Tofu Cubes
Mushroom Broth
Basic Black Beans
Herbed Potatoes
Berry Compote
Slow-téed Onions
Speedy Slow-Cooked Lentils
Slow-Cooked Baked Potatoes
Herbed Brown Rice
BBQ Boss Sauce
Slow-Cooked Quinoa
No-Waste Veggie Broth
Easy Marinara Sauce
Meatless Grounds
Chickpea Buffalo Dip

BAKED BEANS

PREP TIME: 5 MINUTES • **COOK TIME:** 2 TO 3 HOURS ON LOW

GLUTEN-FREE, SOY-FREE

Baked beans are a summer cookout staple. Throw your own pool party and serve up these Baked Beans and a vegan hot dog—and don't forget the veggies. These beans are a great source of protein and have a slight hint of sweetness from the molasses.

---

1 (15-ounce) can low-sodium great northern beans, drained and rinsed

¼ cup diced yellow onion

¼ cup BBQ Boss Sauce or low-sugar barbecue sauce

1 tablespoon vegan Worcestershire sauce

1 tablespoon Dijon mustard

½ tablespoon molasses

1 garlic clove, minced

⅛ teaspoon hot sauce

1. Combine beans, onions, BBQ sauce, Worcestershire sauce, Dijon mustard, molasses, garlic, and hot sauce in a 3-quart slow cooker.
2. Cook on low for 2 to 3 hours, then serve alongside any dish you'd like.

MAKE IT A MEAL:
Complete your meal and serve this with BBQ Jackfruit.

USE IT UP:
Use any extra molasses to add to Vanilla-Berry Oatmeal or make a sauce for the Veggie Fajitas.

SHOP SMART:
Molasses can replace honey or maple syrup.

PER SERVING:
CALORIES: 259; TOTAL FAT: 1G; SATURATED FAT: 0G; PROTEIN: 12G; TOTAL CARBOHYDRATES: 52G; FIBER: 11G; SODIUM: 546MG

GINGER-SESAME TOFU CUBES

PREP TIME: 1 HOUR • **COOK TIME:** 4 TO 6 HOURS ON LOW

GLUTEN-FREE

A solid tofu recipe is a vegan must-have. Ginger-Sesame Tofu Cubes can be added to stir-fry salads or even to a lunch wrap. Packaged tofu has water inside of the container to keep it fresh. To achieve a firm tofu, try to remove as much water as possible by pressing the tofu prior to cooking it or buy a tofu press online. My personal favorite is the Tofuture brand.

- 8 ounces extra-firm tofu
- 2 tablespoons sesame oil
- 2 tablespoons coconut aminos
- 1 tablespoon white miso paste
- 2 teaspoons red chili paste
- 1 teaspoon rice wine vinegar
- ½ teaspoon ground ginger

1. Using a tofu press or two paper-towel-lined plates with a heavy object on top, press the tofu for 1 hour. Cut into bite-size cubes.
2. In a medium bowl, mix the sesame oil, coconut aminos, miso paste, red chili paste, vinegar, and ginger. Set aside.
3. Toss the tofu lightly with the ginger-sesame mixture.

4. Carefully remove the tofu from the marinade and set the cubes in one even layer across the bottom of a 3-quart slow cooker.

5. Cook on low for 4 to 6 hours, or until the tofu reaches your desired texture.

MAKE IT A MEAL:

Try adding this ginger-sesame tofu to Tofu Pad Thai or Simple Soba Noodle Soup .

SHOP SMART:

Extra-firm tofu is best for meals where it's used as a meat replacer, such as stir-fries or curries. Silken tofu is best used for sauces or puddings.

PER SERVING:
CALORIES: 247; TOTAL FAT: 21G; SATURATED FAT: 1G; PROTEIN: 12G; TOTAL CARBOHYDRATES: 4G; FIBER: 3G; SODIUM: 330MG

MUSHROOM BROTH

PREP TIME: 5 MINUTES • **COOK TIME:** 4 HOURS ON LOW

GLUTEN-FREE, SOY-FREE

Mushroom broth is good to have on hand for a variety of different recipes. Use it to make the base of soups or in any recipe that calls for vegetable broth. The more flavorful the broth is, the better tasting the dish will be. The long cook time gives the mushrooms a deep, savory flavor as if they had been sautéed.

---

3 cups low-sodium vegetable broth

2 cups diced portobello mushrooms

1 celery stalk, chopped

1 tablespoon coconut aminos

1 bay leaf

1. Combine the broth, mushrooms, celery, coconut aminos, and bay leaf in a 3-quart slow cooker.
2. Cook on low for 4 hours, or until the broth is nice and steamy!
3. Remove the bay leaf and serve immediately or refrigerate in an airtight container for up to 1 week.

MAKE IT A MEAL:

One of the best ways to use this broth is in Simple Soba Noodle Soup.

USE IT UP:

Use any leftover mushrooms in Creamy Mushroom and Broccoli Risotto.

SHOP SMART:

Try purchasing mushrooms in bulk so you can get just as much as you need.

PER SERVING:
CALORIES: 20; TOTAL FAT: 0G; SATURATED FAT: 0G; PROTEIN: 2G; TOTAL CARBOHYDRATES: 4G; FIBER: 1G; SODIUM: 15MG

BASIC BLACK BEANS

PREP TIME: 5 MINUTES • COOK TIME: 5 HOURS ON HIGH

GLUTEN-FREE, SOY-FREE

Black beans are another must-have vegan staple. Beans are an affordable, easy-to-prepare protein source with vitamins, minerals, and nutrients all in one bite. Dried beans last longer than canned beans and provide more servings per bag for less money. Soaking your beans helps reduce the amount of gas-causing enzymes and makes their protein easier to digest after eating.

---

1 cup water, plus more for soaking

½ cup dried black beans

¼ cup diced onion

1 teaspoon ground cumin

⅛ teaspoon iodized salt

1. Put the beans into a container and cover them with water by about 2 inches. Let them soak for up to 24 hours. Drain the soaking water and rinse the beans with fresh cold water.
2. Combine the water, beans, onions, cumin, and salt in a 3-quart slow cooker.
3. Cook on low for 5 hours, until the beans are tender.

MAKE IT A MEAL:
Beans can go on literally anything. Make this a meal by pairing it with Herbed Brown Rice. Together, rice and beans are a complete protein which makes them unstoppable.

PER SERVING:
CALORIES: 177; TOTAL FAT: 1G; SATURATED FAT: 0G; PROTEIN: 11G; TOTAL CARBOHYDRATES: 33G; FIBER: 8G; SODIUM: 160MG

HERBED POTATOES

PREP TIME: 5 MINUTES • **COOK TIME:** 3 TO 4 HOURS ON LOW

GLUTEN-FREE, SOY-FREE

Fingerling potatoes are a fun shape with a soft texture. Add some herbs, and you have a classic, flavorful side dish. Pair them with a seitan steak to give that "meat and potatoes" feel, then make the other half of the plate vegetables for maximum nutritional value. Cooking with small fingerling potatoes helps with mindful eating. If fingerlings aren't available, any small potatoes will work.

---

2 cups petite fingerling potatoes

¼ cup chopped yellow onion

2 tablespoons dried parsley

1 tablespoon olive oil

1 teaspoon dried thyme

Iodized salt

Freshly ground black pepper

1. Combine the potatoes, onions, parsley, olive oil, thyme, salt, and pepper in a 3-quart slow cooker. Stir to combine.
2. Cook on low for 3 to 4 hours, or until the potatoes are tender.

MAKE IT A MEAL:

Pair these Herbed Potatoes with <u>Slow-Cooked Lentil Loaf</u>.

SHOP SMART:

When shopping at your grocery store, look for a sale produce section for produce that is nearer to its expiration at a heavily discounted rate.

PER SERVING:
CALORIES: 186; TOTAL FAT: 7G; SATURATED FAT: 1G; PROTEIN: 3G; TOTAL CARBOHYDRATES: 29G; FIBER: 4G; SODIUM: 89MG

BERRY COMPOTE

PREP TIME: 5 MINUTES • **COOK TIME:** 1 TO 2 HOURS ON LOW

GLUTEN-FREE, SOY-FREE

This compote is my go-to topping for toast, pancakes, and oatmeal. Traditional maple syrup and jam are often higher in sugar and additives; making this recipe from scratch is easy and much healthier. Strawberries are my favorite, but any berries can be used. The addition of chia seeds increases the omega-3 content and helps create a jam-like texture.

---

1 cup frozen strawberries

¼ cup water

1 tablespoon apple cider vinegar

1 tablespoon chia seeds

1 teaspoon vanilla extract

1. Combine the frozen strawberries, water, vinegar, chia seeds, and vanilla in a 3-quart slow cooker.
2. Cook on low for 1 to 2 hours. Mash the remaining fruit chunks with a potato masher or fork.

MAKE IT A MEAL:

Berry Compote can complete so many meals. Try adding it to Slow-Cooked Pancake or use it to make a PB&J for lunch.

SHOP SMART:

Frozen strawberries are best to purchase when fresh strawberries are out of season. Strawberries are at the peak of their harvest in June.

PER SERVING:
CALORIES: 81; TOTAL FAT: 2G; SATURATED FAT: 0G; PROTEIN: 2G; TOTAL CARBOHYDRATES: 13G; FIBER: 5G; SODIUM: 4MG

SLOW-TÉED ONIONS

PREP TIME: 5 MINUTES • **COOK TIME:** 8 TO 10 HOURS ON LOW

GLUTEN-FREE, SOY-FREE, SET-AND-FORGET

Slow-cooked onions taste just as good as sautéed onions. Cooking the onions for 8 to 10 hours gives them a perfect caramelization. Use these onions in fajitas or soups. If you are unable to find yellow onions—or have another type already in your pantry—feel free to slow cook them instead.

---

1 pound sliced yellow onion

1 tablespoon olive oil

1. Combine the onions and olive oil in a 3-quart slow cooker and mix until the onions are coated.
2. Cook on low for 8 to 10 hours.

MAKE IT A MEAL:

Use these Slow-téed Onions as the base of French Onion Soup or add them to Simple Tofu Scramble.

SHOP SMART:

When shopping for onions, choose firm onions with dry, paper-like skin. Avoid ones that have soft or brown spots.

PER SERVING:
CALORIES: 150; TOTAL FAT: 7G; SATURATED FAT: 1G; PROTEIN: 2G; TOTAL

CARBOHYDRATES: 21G; FIBER: 4G; SODIUM: 9MG

SPEEDY SLOW-COOKED LENTILS

PREP TIME: 5 MINUTES • COOK TIME: 1 HOUR ON HIGH

GLUTEN-FREE, SOY-FREE

Lentils are another plant-based protein. Like beans, they are part of the legume family. Green lentils are especially good at holding their shape when cooked (red lentils can get mushy). Sprouted green lentils are another good option. When legumes are sprouted, it makes them easier for the body to break them down and extract their nutrients.

---

1 cup low-sodium vegetable broth

½ cup dried green lentils

¼ cup diced onion

1 garlic clove, minced

1. Combine the broth, lentils, onions, and garlic in a 3-quart slow cooker.
2. Cover and cook on high for 1 hour, or until the lentils are tender.

MAKE IT A MEAL:

Lentils work wonders in many meals and can be combined with Meatless Grounds to increase the total amount of fiber.

USE IT UP:
Use up any extra lentils in Slow-Cooked Lentil Loaf or Red Lentil-Coconut Dal.

PER SERVING:
CALORIES: 179; TOTAL FAT: 1G; SATURATED FAT: 0G; PROTEIN: 12G; TOTAL CARBOHYDRATES: 34G; FIBER: 6G; SODIUM: 4MG

SLOW-COOKED BAKED POTATOES

PREP TIME: 5 MINUTES • **COOK TIME:** 4 TO 5 HOURS ON HIGH

GLUTEN-FREE, SOY-FREE

You can't go wrong adding a baked potato to your meal. With the outside a little crisp and the inside soft and fluffy, a baked potato is the perfect combination of textures. They can also be loaded up with any of your favorite ingredients to make a full meal. Russet potatoes are ideal for this recipe because of their oblong size and thick skin. Try using this recipe as a base for potato boats or potato tacos.

---

2 whole russet potatoes

½ tablespoon olive oil

Iodized salt

Freshly ground black pepper

1. Wash and scrub the potatoes well, then poke holes all over each potato with a fork. Sprinkle each potato with olive oil, salt, and pepper.
2. Wrap the potatoes tightly with aluminum foil and place them in the bottom of a 3-quart slow cooker.
3. Cook on high for 4 to 5 hours, or until the potatoes are tender.

MAKE IT A MEAL:
Add a baked potato to <u>Chickpea Noodle Soup</u> when you're not feeling well, or to <u>Vegan Not–Pot Roast</u> for a hearty, filling meal.

SHOP SMART:
Purchase russet potatoes in bulk bags for maximum cost efficiency.

PER SERVING:
CALORIES: 198; TOTAL FAT: 4G; SATURATED FAT: 1G; PROTEIN: 5G; TOTAL CARBOHYDRATES: 38G; FIBER: 3G; SODIUM: 88MG

HERBED BROWN RICE

PREP TIME: 5 MINUTES • **COOK TIME:** 1 HOUR 30 MINUTES TO 2 HOURS ON HIGH

GLUTEN-FREE, SOY-FREE

This recipe is a savory take on brown rice that uses dried herbs and spices. Long-grain rice has less starch and, when cooked, the grains remain separate from each other, making it ideal to mix with aromatic herbs. Combining thyme, sage, and rosemary creates a perfect herb blend that is reminiscent of a Thanksgiving meal. But you can pair this dish with almost anything; feel free to change the herbs and spices to match the cuisine.

1½ cups low-sodium vegetable broth

1 cup long-grain brown rice

1 tablespoon olive oil

½ teaspoon dried thyme

½ teaspoon dried rosemary

¼ teaspoon dried sage

1. Combine the broth, rice, olive oil, thyme, rosemary, and sage in a 3-quart slow cooker.
2. Cook on high for 1 hour 30 minutes to 2 hours, or until the rice is cooked through.

MAKE IT A MEAL:
Add this rice to Veggie Fajitas or Very Veggie Enchiladas.

PER SERVING:
CALORIES: 404; TOTAL FAT: 10G; SATURATED FAT: 2G; PROTEIN: 7G; TOTAL CARBOHYDRATES: 72G; FIBER: 4G; SODIUM: 7MG

BBQ BOSS SAUCE

PREP TIME: 5 MINUTES • **COOK TIME:** 3 HOURS ON LOW

SOY-FREE

The best sauce in town is definitely barbecue sauce! This is my great-great-grandmother's recipe which dates back to the 1920s. It was kept safe in a recipe box with three other recipes that survived. After Prohibition, she loved to put whiskey in everything. Not all alcohol is vegan; in this case, you can use Jameson Irish Whiskey. I made some modern-day modifications, but this recipe is close to its true form. It can be used on meatballs, cauliflower wings, or just as a general dipping sauce. Give it a try in the new roaring '20s.

⅓ cup no-sugar-added ketchup

¼ cup vegan Worcestershire sauce

¼ cup water

¼ cup freshly squeezed lemon juice

¼ cup apple cider vinegar

2 tablespoons olive oil

2 tablespoons whiskey

2 tablespoons Tabasco sauce

1 teaspoon paprika

1 garlic clove, minced

1. Combine the ketchup, Worcestershire sauce, water, lemon juice, vinegar, oil, whiskey, tabasco sauce, paprika, and garlic in a 3-quart slow cooker and mix well.
2. Cook on low for 3 hours, then enjoy!

MAKE IT A MEAL:

Spice up Easy Bean Balls with this BBQ Boss Sauce.

PER SERVING:
CALORIES: 238; TOTAL FAT: 14G; SATURATED FAT: 2G; PROTEIN: 1G; TOTAL CARBOHYDRATES: 21G; FIBER: 1G; SODIUM: 791MG

SLOW-COOKED QUINOA

PREP TIME: 5 MINUTES • **COOK TIME:** 3 TO 4 HOURS ON LOW

GLUTEN-FREE, SOY-FREE

Quinoa can be hard to get just right on the stove. This recipe takes the hassle out of making grains; simply add all the ingredients to a slow cooker and let it do its thing. No need to worry about forgetting to turn the stove off or not adding enough water. Quinoa comes in two main colors—tricolor and regular white. Both cook the same in this recipe. Make quinoa on Sunday to have throughout the week and add it to Mediterranean bowls or a big bowl of greens.

---

2 cups low-sodium vegetable broth or water

1 cup quinoa

⅛ teaspoon iodized salt

1. Combine the broth, quinoa, and salt in a 3-quart slow cooker.
2. Cook on low for 3 to 4 hours. Cook times may vary depending on your slow cooker, so when making for the first time, keep an eye on yours. The final texture should be soft and fluffy.

MAKE IT A MEAL:

Quinoa is a whole grain and makes a great addition to salads or as a side for almost any meal. One-fourth of your plate at meals should be a complex carbohydrate and quinoa qualifies perfectly.

PER SERVING:
CALORIES: 313; TOTAL FAT: 5G; SATURATED FAT: 1G; PROTEIN: 12G; TOTAL CARBOHYDRATES: 54G; FIBER: 6G; SODIUM: 159MG

NO-WASTE VEGGIE BROTH

PREP TIME: 5 MINUTES • **COOK TIME:** 8 TO 10 HOURS ON LOW

GLUTEN-FREE, SOY-FREE, SET-AND-FORGET

No more tossing kitchen scraps! This No-Waste Veggie Broth will give your scraps a second life. Using broth is a great way to add extra flavor to rice, lentils, soups, and any other dish that calls for water. Some great scraps to include are onion skins, garlic, carrot tops, celery leaves, leeks, herb stems, pepper stems, kale stems, mushrooms, and more.

---

4 cups vegetable scraps

4 cups water

1. Once you have your scraps collected, add them along with the water to a 3-quart slow cooker. Don't worry about thawing the vegetables; they can go in frozen.
2. Cook for 8 to 10 hours on low.
3. Once the cook time is finished, strain the broth so that only the liquid remains. You can add additional spices or herbs, such as salt, pepper, or thyme, once everything is strained as desired.
4. Store the broth in the refrigerator for up to 1 week or freeze for up to 6 months.

MAKE IT A MEAL:
No-Waste Veggie Broth goes great with any soups, especially Chickpea Noodle Soup.

SHOP SMART:
Keep a baggie of scraps in your freezer; this prevents them from going bad and gives you time to collect enough to make a batch of broth.

PER SERVING:
CALORIES:10; TOTAL FAT: 0G; SATURATED FAT: 0G; PROTEIN: 0G; TOTAL CARBOHYDRATES: 2G; FIBER: 0G; SODIUM: 2MG

EASY MARINARA SAUCE

PREP TIME: 5 MINUTES • **COOK TIME:** 8 HOURS ON LOW

GLUTEN-FREE, SOY-FREE

Marinara sauce is excellent for game day meatballs or homemade pizzas. Created from a blend of tomatoes and spices, this recipe is a great way to sneak in an extra serving of vegetables. Another trick that works especially well with kids is to blend vegetables like spinach into the sauce once it's done cooking. They'll never know!

2 (28-ounce) cans crushed tomatoes

1 (6-ounce) can tomato paste

½ cup diced onion

1 tablespoon dried basil

1 tablespoon balsamic vinegar

2 teaspoons dried oregano

1 garlic clove, minced

½ teaspoon freshly ground black pepper

2 whole bay leaves

1. Combine the tomatoes, tomato paste, onions, basil, vinegar, oregano, garlic, pepper, and bay leaves in a 3-quart slow cooker.
2. Cook the sauce on low for 8 hours.

3. Once the cooking time is finished, remove the bay leaves and serve.

MAKE IT A MEAL:
Use this as a base for <u>Spaghetti Squash Marinara</u> or on homemade pizza!

SHOP SMART:
When shopping for herbs like bay leaves, examine them closely before buying to ensure the leaves are a rich green color.

PER SERVING:
CALORIES: 227; TOTAL FAT: 3G; SATURATED FAT: 0G; PROTEIN: 11G; TOTAL CARBOHYDRATES: 50G; FIBER: 20G; SODIUM: 212MG

MEATLESS GROUNDS

PREP TIME: 5 MINUTES • **COOK TIME:** 1 TO 2 HOURS ON LOW

GLUTEN-FREE

Ground meat was one of my favorite foods growing up. It can be used in almost any dish and adds great texture and flavor. Textured vegetable protein is an affordable vegan protein that makes for a fabulous substitute. Not only is it affordable, but the texture is remarkable.

---

1 cup low-sodium vegetable broth

2 tablespoons tomato paste

1 tablespoon coconut aminos

1 tablespoon vegan Worcestershire sauce

1 teaspoon ground cumin

1 teaspoon onion powder

1 teaspoon liquid smoke (optional)

1 cup textured vegetable protein

Iodized salt

Freshly ground black pepper

1. In a small bowl, combine the vegetable broth, tomato paste, coconut aminos, Worcestershire sauce, cumin, onion powder, and liquid smoke (if using). Mix well.

2. Add the textured vegetable protein to the bowl and stir to coat. Once everything is combined, add the mixture to a 3-quart slow cooker.

3. Cook on low for 1 to 2 hours. Season with salt and pepper, as desired.

MAKE IT A MEAL:

Add Meatless Grounds to <u>Lentil Bolognese</u> or <u>Cajun Red Beans and Rice</u>.

SHOP SMART:

Buy textured vegetable protein from the bulk section to get more bang for your buck. If shopping in the aisles, packaged versions can be found with the flours, flaxseed, and chia seeds.

PER SERVING:
CALORIES: 140; TOTAL FAT: 0G; SATURATED FAT: 0G; PROTEIN: 19G; TOTAL CARBOHYDRATES: 18G; FIBER: 7G; SODIUM: 95MG

CHICKPEA BUFFALO DIP

PREP TIME: 10 MINUTES • COOK TIME: 3 TO 4 HOURS ON LOW

GLUTEN-FREE, SOY-FREE

This spicy dip is delicious with vegetables or chips and is a must-have for Sunday night football. When I was in school to become a dietitian, my roommate made a chickpea buffalo dip I loved. I lost the recipe but recreated it here from memory.

---

1 (15-ounce) can white beans, drained and rinsed

1 cup raw cashews

1 (15-ounce) can low-sodium chickpeas, drained and rinsed

¾ cup hot sauce

½ cup nondairy milk

2 tablespoons nutritional yeast

1 tablespoon freshly squeezed lemon juice

1 garlic clove, minced

1 teaspoon paprika

1 teaspoon onion powder

1. Blend the white beans and cashews together in a blender or food processor.

2. Once blended, transfer the mixture to a 3-quart slow cooker. Then, mix in the chickpeas, hot sauce, milk, nutritional yeast, lemon juice, garlic, paprika, and onion powder until well combined.

3. Cook on low for 3 to 4 hours, or until nice and creamy. Enjoy!

MAKE IT A MEAL:

Spread this spicy bean dip on a wrap or pita, or place a dollop of it on a nourishing grain bowl or Very Veggie Enchiladas.

SHOP SMART:

Buying dried beans and cooking them in batches is much more cost-effective than repeatedly buying cans.

PER SERVING:
CALORIES: 739; TOTAL FAT: 37G; SATURATED FAT: 6G; PROTEIN: 33G; TOTAL CARBOHYDRATES: 79G; FIBER: 11G; SODIUM: 834MG

APPLE CIDER

Measurement Conversions

VOLUME EQUIVALENTS (LIQUID)

US STANDARD	US STANDARD (OUNCES)	METRIC (APPROXIMATE)
2 tablespoons	1 fl. oz.	30 mL
¼ cup	2 fl. oz.	60 mL
½ cup	4 fl. oz.	120 mL
1 cup	8 fl. oz.	240 mL
1½ cups	12 fl. oz.	355 mL
2 cups or 1 pint	16 fl. oz.	475 mL
4 cups or 1 quart	32 fl. oz.	1 L
1 gallon	128 fl. oz.	4 L

OVEN TEMPERATURES

FAHRENHEIT (F)	CELSIUS (C) (APPROXIMATE)
250°F	120°C
300°F	150°C
325°F	165°C
350°F	180°C
375°F	190°C
400°F	200°C
425°F	220°C
450°F	230°C

VOLUME EQUIVALENTS (DRY)

US STANDARD	METRIC (APPROXIMATE)
⅛ teaspoon	0.5 mL
¼ teaspoon	1 mL
½ teaspoon	2 mL
¾ teaspoon	4 mL
1 teaspoon	5 mL
1 tablespoon	15 mL
¼ cup	59 mL
⅓ cup	79 mL
½ cup	118 mL
⅔ cup	156 mL
¾ cup	177 mL
1 cup	235 mL
2 cups or 1 pint	475 mL
3 cups	700 mL
4 cups or 1 quart	1 L

WEIGHT EQUIVALENTS

US STANDARD	METRIC (APPROXIMATE)
½ ounce	15 g
1 ounce	30 g
2 ounces	60 g
4 ounces	115 g
8 ounces	225 g
12 ounces	340 g
16 ounces or 1 pound	455 g

Printed in Great Britain
by Amazon